AF600503

THE CATHOLIC UNIVERSITY OF AMERICA
CANON LAW STUDIES
No. 339

The Parish Census and the Liber Status Animarum

A HISTORICAL SYNOPSIS AND A COMMENTARY

A DISSERTATION

Submitted to the Faculty of the School of Canon Law of the Catholic University of America in Partial Fulfillment of the Requirements for the Degree of Doctor of Canon Law

by

REV. WILLIAM FRANCIS FITZGERALD, A.B., S.T.L., J.C.L.
Priest of the Diocese of Trenton

THE CATHOLIC UNIVERSITY OF AMERICA PRESS
WASHINGTON, D. C.
1954

NIHIL OBSTAT:

CLEMENS V. BASTNAGEL, J.U.D., S.T.L.

Censor Deputatus

Washingtonii, D.C. die 12 decembris 1953

IMPRIMATUR:

✠ GEORGIUS G. AHR, S.T.D.

Episcopus Trentonensis

Trentonii, die 18 decembris 1953

PRINTED BY

NEW JERSEY'S BOYSTOWN PRESS

ARLINGTON, NEW JERSEY

TABLE OF CONTENTS

PART III. CANONICAL COMMENTARY

CHAPTER VI

CHAPTER VII

CHAPTER VIII

CHAPTER IX

FOREWORD

A pious and zealous priesthood is the glory of the Church of God. By personal holiness, the priest works out his own salvation and edifies his flock; by his zeal, he makes men partakers of the precious heritage of Christ. This zeal has been expressed in many ways throughout the history of the Church, but experience shows that if it is really to be effective the priest must have an intimate knowledge of his flock. Such knowledge he can acquire by means of a parish census and through the use of the *liber status animarum.*

In the following pages the writer has attempted first to present a clear notion of the concepts of the parish census and the *liber status animarum.* This is followed by a historical review of these entities, beginning with the foundation of the Church by our divine Savior and ending with the promulgation of the Code of Canon Law. Many notions, at first only implicit, received a well-defined and explicit form in the course of time. The treatment is arranged according to the commonly accepted periods in the history of Canon Law, a special emphasis being laid on what little general legislation was to be found. The third part of this work is concerned with present canonical legislation on both the census and the *liber status animarum.* Treated accordingly are the matter to be included in the census and the *liber status animarum,* the persons to be listed in these entities, the obligation to take the census and to keep the *liber,* and the manner in which they are to be taken and kept.

The writer wishes at this time to express his gratitude to his Excellency, the Most Reverend George W. Ahr, S. T. D., Bishop of Trenton, for the opportunity to pursue advanced studies in Canon Law and for his kind generosity in making this publication possible; to the members of the Faculty of the School of Canon Law for their devoted assistance; and to all who have helped in anyway whatsoever in the preparation of this dissertation.

He dedicates this work to Mary Immaculate, Mother alike to the Divine Shepherd and His flock.

PRELIMINARY DISCUSSION

CHAPTER I

Preliminary Notions

Article I: The Parish Census

a) Relation to canon 467

Though the Code of Canon Law does not contain an explicit prescription concerning the parish census, it does require pastors to become acquainted with the people living in their parishes. ***Debet parochus. . suas oves cognoscere.***[1] Such a directive, however, almost of necessity, implies the use of the parish census, especially for the gaining of a complete knowledge of each and every parishioner.

With the decline of the parish church and rectory as the center of Catholic life in the community, fewer and fewer Catholics come into direct contact with the priest.[2] Such diversions as the radio, television, motion pictures, and automobile have taken their toll. Moreover, no longer do Catholics rely exclusively on the priest, who was once the only one to whom they could turn in their hour of need.[3] Agencies—social, political, and non-religious—though in many ways good, have risen to stand between the priest and the people. Then, too, the growth of large cities, with parishes containing thousands of families, make the ever-so-important personal contact, and hence an intimate understanding, between the priest and his flock a physical impossibility.[4] These are but a few of the more

[1] Canon, 467, 1—Debet parochus officia divina celebrare, administrare Sacramenta fidelibus, quoties legitime petant, suas oves cognoscere et errantes prudenter corrigere, pauperes ac miseros paterna caritate complecti, maximam curam adhibere in catholica puerorum institutione.

[2] J. Peterson, "Knowng Our Own," *The Ecclesiastical Reveew* (Vols. XXXIII-CIX, Philadelphia, 1905-1943), LXXXVIII (1933), 295 (hereafter cited ER). Up to 1905 and since 1944: *The American Eccletical Review* (to be cited *AER.*)

[3] G Kelly, "The Parish Census," *The Sociology of the Parish,* ed. by C. H. Nuesse and T. J. Harte, C. Ss. R. (Milwaukee: The Bruce Publishing Co., 1951), p. 237.

[4] Anon., "The Parish That Came Back," *ER,* LXI (1919), 27.

obvious reasons why, if the regulation of canon 467, 1. is to be followed, namely that the pastor is to know his flock, a parish census is called for and is necessary.

b) Definition (including purpose)

The word census itself, derived as it is from the Latin *censure,* points to an act of evaluation,[5] and from ancient Roman times was applied to a numbering of the people and an evaluation of their estates for a twofold purpose, the first that of taxation, and the second that of determining the position of citizens in the Servian armies.[6] While the purpose could vary according to the institution conducting the census, the underlying meaning was ever present, namely, to evaluate. Civil governments generally enumerate the population of their country, a city, or town for social and economic reasons: to apportion the number of representatives in the central government, to learn of the mortality and birth rates, living conditions, average yearly income, etc.[7]

What, then, is the purpose of the *parish* census? This question must be answered before any formulation of a strict definition is possible.

In general it may be said that a parish census may have any one of three purposes; the compilation of membership statistics, the provision of data for scientific research, or the diagnosis and correction of the religious condition of the parish.[8] The first mentioned, the statistical census, in itself is obviously insufficient. This type aims at the accumulation of numbers. It emphasizes names and addresses. While the results may be handy for statistical reports as found in the Catholic Directory, it merely names and numbers the known Catholics and, as such, is of little value.[9]

[5]. *Webster's Collegiate Dictionary* (5. ed., Springfield, Mass.: G. & C. Merriam Company, 1943), p. 164.

[6] R. W. Leage, *Roman Private Law* (2. ed. by C. H. Ziegler, London: MacMillan and Company, 1930; reprint, 1948) pp. 56-58.

[7]F. A. Ogg and P. O. Ray, *Introduction to American Government* (9.ed., New York: Appleton—Century—Crofts, Inc., 1948) p. 638; cf. S. Chase, "What the New Census Means." *Public Affairs Pamphlets,* No. 56 (New York, 1941); cf. The Constitution of the United States, Art. I, Sec. II, Parag. III.

[8] C. Nuesse—T. Harte, *The Sociology of the Parish,* p. 234.

[9] A. H. Clemens, "The Need for Constructive Thinking in Sociological

The second, the research census, while mainly of importance to professional sociologists and Catholic agencies, is much closer to the true parish census. This enumeration of the Catholic population is made with a view to a scientific study of the fertility and mortality rates among Catholics, the effect of mixed marriages, Catholic education, etc.[10] The information thereby garnered is of use in a long-range program of mitigating harmful material and spiritual conditions among Catholics as well as of strengthening their faith and devotion. For these reasons the research census has definite value.

However, from the Church's point of view, the third, namely the therapeutic census, is the only real parish census. In regard to this, a letter written under the direction of the Holy See by the Apostolic Delegate to all the Bishops of the United States has particular importance. In part it reads:

> The Holy See has often noted with interest how much is accomplished for the welfare of souls in this country through the zealous use of statistical data . . . To make the pastoral ministry by this means ever more fruitful. the Sacred Congregation of the Council has instructed me to remind the Bishops of this country of their obligation to have parish priests keep an accurate and current census of the faithful entrusted to their care.[11]

Clear, then, is the mind of the Church in regard to the purpose of the parish census. That purpose is the welfare of souls. The census aims at an *immediate* correction, or at least at a lessening, of conditions harmful to spiritual progress, and at an *immediate* in-

Research," *The American Catholic Sociological Review* (Chicago, Ill., Loyola University), I (1940), 75.

[10] Cf. Gerald J. Schnepp, S. M., *Leakage from a Catholic Parish* (Kirkwood, Mo.: Maryhurst Press, 1942) ; Thomas F. Coogan, *Catholic Fertility in Florida* (Washington, D. C., The Catholic University of America Press, 1946).

[11] Letter of the Apostolic Delegate, June 12, 1941—T. L. Bouscaren, *The Canon Law Digest* (2 vols. and Supplement through 1948, Milwaukee: The Bruce Publishing Company, 1934, 1943, 1949), II, 147 (hereafter cited *Digest*).

[11] Letter of the Apostolic Delegate, June 12, 1941—T. L. Bousearen, *The Canon Law Digest* (2 vols. and Supplement through 1948, Milwaukee: The Bruce Publishing Company, 1934, 1943, 1949), II, 147 (hereafter cited *Digest*).

crease in faith and devotion.[12] More explicitly, the pastor should take the census in order to reclaim the lost sheep, to validate invalid marriages, to convert the unconverted, to instruct the ignorant, and to lead the lukewarm and indifferent back to the sacraments.

Among the duties of a pastor mentioned in the Code of Canon Law one finds that he is to correct prudently those who are in error, assist with paternal charity the poor and the suffering, instruct the children in their religious obligations,[13] prepare the sick for a happy death,[14] and, in general, to stand vigilant lest anything contrary to faith and morals springs up in his parish.[15] How is all of this possible if he does not know the ones who are in error, the poor and the suffering, the children and the sick? Properly to fulfill his duties the pastor must know his people.

In the Parable of the Good Shepherd, Christ gave an indication of the knowledge required in a model pastor of his flock: "I am the good shepherd," He said, "and I know mine, and mine know me, even as the Father knoweth me, and I know the Father."[16] Christ thus taught the ideal after which the ministry is to be fashioned, and that ideal is nothing less than that intimate, perfect knowledge which the Father has of the Son, and the Son of the Father.[17] Living with his sheep constantly, the shepherd knows them all intimately. "He calleth his own sheep by name," says the Gospel.[18]

Such knowledge, though, is not to be merely speculative. Witness the further statements of Sacred Scripture. At nightfall the good shepherd numbers them one by one to make sure that none are missing. "The flocks shall pass again under the hand of him that numbereth

[12] *Sociology of the Parish,* p. 235.

[13] Canon 467, 1; cf. *supra,* Note 1.

[14] Canon 468, 1.—Sedula cura et effusa caritate debet parochus aegrotos in sua paroecia, maxime vero morti proximos, adiuvare, eos sollicite Sacramentis reficiendo eorumque animas Deo commendando.

[15] Canon 469.—Parochus diligenter advigilet ne quid contra fidem ac mores in sua paroecia, praesertim in scholis publicis et privatis, tradatur, et opera caritatis, fidei ac pietatis foveat aut instituat.

[16] St. John, X: 14, 15.

[17] The Catholic Biblical Association, *A Commentary on the New Testament* (Kansas City: William Sadlier, Inc., 1942), p. 330.

[18] St. John, X: 3.

them."[19] "He will seek that which was lost: and that which was driven away, he will bring back again: and he will bind up that which was broken, and he will strengthen that which was weak, and that which was fat and strong he will preserve: and he will feed them in judgement."[20] Such then is the knowledge required of a pastor. It must be complete, intimate and practical.

In the light of this discussion of the object of the parish census, it is now possible to formulate a definition. The parish census is, in the strict sense, *an act by which all who reside in a parish are enumerated with a view to determining the moral and religious condition of the parish and with the intention of correcting existing moral evils.*[21] It is basically an action, namely the gathering of information.

Article II: *The Liber Status Animarum*

a) Relation to canon 470

It is in this point that the difference between the parish census and the *liber status animarum* is to be noted. The census is an action, the *liber status animarum* the result of that action. It is the book in which is recorded the information gained through census-taking.[22] It is not a mere compilation of the baptismal, marriage, confirmation, and death registers, though some of the material contained in these books overlap that which is to be found in the *liber status animarum.* The later contains rather an up-to-date account of the spiritual condition of each soul within a parish in its quest for God. It is the record of each man's progress through the sacramental system and his use of other means of grace.

[19] Jeremias, XXXIII: 13

[20] Ezechiel, XXXIV: 16.

[21] Walter Wilcox, "Census," *Encyclopedia of the Social Sciences,* III, 295-300.

[22] J. O'Rourke, *Parish Registers,* The Catholic University of America Canon Law Studies, n. 88 (Washington, D. C.: The Catholic University of America, 1934), pp. 82-84.

Canon 470 of the Code of Canon Law,[23] in treating of the parochial books which are to be maintained and preserved by all pastors, specifically mentions *the liber status animarum* as one. *Parochus . . . etiam librum de statu animarum accurate conficere pro viribus curet.*

b) English terminology

For the sake of clarity, it seems called for at this time to find an English equivalent for the term *"liber status animarum."* Authors who have written commentaries on the Code in the English language are not at one in their choice of terms. Augustine (1872 - 1943) used the expression "taking an accurate census of parishioners."[24] Abbo-Hannan refer to it as a "register of the spiritual condition of the members of a parish."[25] Bouscaren-Ellis identify it with "the parish census,"[26] while Ayrinhac (1867-1930)[27] and Woywod (1880-1941)-Smith[28] employed the term "census book." All except Abbo-Hannan and Woywod-Smith in subsequent passages lapse into the Latin, apparently dissatified with their own attempted translation. This lack of uniformity in the choice of an English term corresponding to the Latin terminology readily shows the difficulty of finding an appropriate and, at the same time, a suitable phrase for the expression used in the Code.

[23] Canon 470, 1—Habeat parochus libros paroeciales: idest librum baptizatorum, confirmatorum, matrimoniorum, defunctorum: etiam librum de statu animarum accurate conficere pro viribus curet; et omnes hos libros, secundum usum ab Ecclesia probatum vel a proprio Ordinario praescriptum, conscribat ac diligenter asservet.

[24] *A Commentary on the New Code of Canon Law* (8 vols., Vol. II, 3. ed., St. Louis, Mo.: B. Herder Book Co., 1919), II, 557 (hereafter cited *Commentary*).

[25] *The Sacred Canons, A Concise Presentation of the Current Disciplinary Norms of the Church* (2 vols. St. Louis: B. Herder Book Co., 1952), I, 466 (hereafter cited *The Sacred Canons*).

[26] Canon Law, A Text and Commentary (Milwaukee: The Bruce Publishing Company, 1948), p. 216 (hereafter cited *Canon Law.*)

[27] *Penal Legislation in the New Code* (Cincinnati: Benzinger Bros., 1920) p. 346.

[28] *A Practical Commentary on the Code of Canon Law* (New York: Joseph F. Wagner, Inc., 1948), I, 195 (hereafter cited *A Practical Commentary*).

To appropriate the Latin terminology seems commendable only when no English equivalent can be found in its place. To use the expression offered by Augustine, identifying it with the parish census, creates ambiguity, and hence confuses the issue. The taking of the census and the keeping of the *liber status animarum* are entirely distinct, as has already been explained, and must be kept so. For the same reason ought the terms used by Bouscaren-Ellis to be avoided. To adopt the appellation "census book" has validity, but it fails to give the full meaning of what is involved. To follow the usage of Abbo-Hannan in calling it "a register of the spiritual condition of the members of a parish" is most commendable, for it is most accurate. Because of this fact, though, it is more of a definition, and as such becomes perhaps unduly lengthy for easy usage. Nevertheless it suggests the expression which this writer proposes to offer. The "parochial spiritual status register" appears to be a satisfactory rendition of the Latin: *liber status animarum.* The hope that this selection will furnish the requisite clarity and exactness of expression prompts its constant use henceforth throughout the present treatise.

c) Definition (including purpose)

The primary purpose motivating legislation on the parish registers in general is the matter of proof.[29] Both the records themselves and the certificates drawn therefrom are public ecclesiastical documents.[30] As such they have full value as proof concerning the things

[29] O'Rourke, *Parish Registers,* p. 5.

[30] Canon 1813, 1.—Praecipua documenta publica ecclesiastica haec sunt: 1° Acta Summi Pontificis et Curiae Romanae et Ordinariorum in exercitio suorum munerum authentica forma exarata, itemque attestationes authenticae de iisdem actibus datae ab llis vel eorum notariis; 2° Instrumenta a notariis ecclesiasticis confecta; 3° Acta iudicialia ecclesiastica; 4° Inscriptiones baptismi, confirmationis, ordinationis, professionis religiosae, matrimonii, mortis, quae habentur in regestis. Curiae vel paroeciae, vel religionis, et attestationes scriptae ex iisdem desumptae et a parchis, vel Ordinariis vel notariis ecclesiasticis confectae aut earum exemplaria authentica.
Canon 1814.—Documenta publica sive ecclesiastica sive civilia genuina praesumuntur, donec contrarium evidentibus argumentis evincatur.

directly and principally set forth in their contents.[31] Their public nature arises from the fact that they are made by a person constituted and acting as a public official,[32] and in a form determined by law.[33] The ecclesiastical nature of the same records is obvious enough, since they contain evidence of the performance of certain ecclesiastical functions.[34] Hence it is apparent that the precise status of the members of the society of the Church can be demonstrated through the use of these authentic records. They give evidence concerning the administration of the sacraments and trace the advancement of the members through the various stages of progress possible in the Church.[35]

However, the parochial spiritual status register is a peculiar one by nature. It is, as previously implied, ***a current record of each parishioner's external status in the Church involving the reception of the sacraments and the use of other means of grace, both spiritual and material, which is kept by all pastors to facilitate the better care of the souls under their guidance.*** Unlike the registers of the baptized, confirmed, married, and deceased, mentioned in the Code, its purpose is of no great legal value.[36] The reason is evident. The information contained therein is not the result of an officiating priest's personal knowledge, but comes from the subject himself. Nevertheless, it must not be thought that this fact vitiates the value of such a register.

[31] Canon 1816.—Documenta publica fidem faciunt de iis quae directe et principaliter in eisdem affirmantur.

[32] A. Veermersch—J. Creusen, *Epitome Iuris Canonici* (4 ed., 3 vols., Mechliniae—Romae: H. Dessain, 1929-1931) III, 77 (hereafter cited *Epitome*); S. C. C., July 3, 1909, n. I — *Acta Apostolicae Sedis* (*AAS*), I (1909), 658: The Sacred Congregation of the Council decided that the pastor acts as a notary when he enters inscriptions in his parochial books from his own personal knowledge or draws certificates from his own parochial registers, but not in other cases, e.g., when entering a record in his register from a certificate drawn elsewhere.

[33] Canons 470, 777, 798, etc.

[34] Vermeersch-Creusen, Epitome, III, 78.

[35] A. Blat, *Commentarium Textus Codicis Iuris Canonici* (5 vols in 6, Romae: Ex Typographia Pontificia in Instituto Pii X, 1919-1927), II, 505.

[36] O'Rourke, *Parish Registers,* p. 82; Aichner, *Compendium Iuris Ecclesiastici* (6 ed., Brixinae, 1887), p. 433; Reiffenstuel, *Ius Canonicum Universum* (7 vols., Parisiis, 1864-1870), III, 102.

The human mind, being what it is, is subject to lapses of memory. In parishes of any size it would be quite impossible for the pastor to remember offhand the exact status of all the souls in his care. For this reason alone a record should be kept in writing. Moreover, should a pastor die or be transferred, such a record would be invaluable to the incoming pastor. After a few hours of continuous study of the spiritual status register the type of pastoral work required of him would become evident, and cases demanding his immediate attention could be handled without delay.[37]

[37] G. Shaughnessy, S. M., "Catholic Statistics and the *Status Animarum* Record," *ER,* C (1939), 98.

HISTORICAL DEVELOPMENT

CHAPTER II

Earliest Years of the Church

Though many references are made to censuses throughout the whole of Sacred Scripture,[1] it is of interest to note that in each case the census was taken, not for religious purposes, but by the civil government for reasons of its own. However, it was only natural for the Church, even in its infancy, to make use of this centuries old process by which it could number its gains in membership and note its material progress. Evidence that this was the case is had in the diptychs.[2] It must be understood though that the census then simply coincided with an enumeration of the Christians. The parish census and parochial spiritual status register as they exist today are of a much later development.

To understand this development postulates an understanding of the parish, with which it is inextricably associated, for a parish census presupposes the existence of a parish.

Article I: Development of The Parish

Since many excellent works have already been written about the historical development of this institute, the treatment afforded here will take the form of a general rather than a detailed presentation, and will serve merely as a brief but necessary background for the subject under discussion. Suffice it to say that in the earliest days of the Church parishes were non-existent. Communities, however, were formed: Judea, Galilee, and Samaria, dependent at the start on Jerusalem; Antioch, Greece, and Asia Minor, under St. Paul; Rome, under Peter; but the authors are in general agreement

1 Eg., II Kings, XXIV:1-2; St. Luke, II:1-3; Acts, V:37

2 Cf. *infra*, p. 14 ff

that there did not exist separate parishes among these communities at least during the first three centuries.[3]

During that period the so-called parish and the diocese were coextensive. Originally having but one church, the diocese began in the second and third centuries to include oratories or places of devotion and prayer.[4] Nevertheless it was only at the bishop's church that mass was celebrated, and it was directly on the bishop that the faithful depended for ministrations.[5] Occasionally duties were delegated to the priests, but pastors as such were unknown.[6]

The Edict of Tolerance, which ended the persecutions when it was issued in the year 313 at Milan, effected a tremendous change. Under Emperor Constantine (d. 337) this edict granted the Christian Church equality of rights with other religions, and in a relatively short time, namely under Theodosius I (379-395), Christianity became for all practical purposes the state religion. It was in the year 381 that the Emperor issued orders forbidding any Christian to join the ranks of the pagans, and made acts of divination punishable by law. This abolished, at one stroke, the most attractive aspect of idolatrous rites. In 391, he took the decisive step of forbidding persons to enter pagan temples under pain of fine, and a year later gave all the ancient temples to the Christians.[7] Numerous conversions followed, and therewith came new problems. Churches

[3] L. Thomassinus, *Vetus et Nova ecclesiae Disciplina* (10 vols., Magontiaci, 1787), Pars. I, Lib. II, Cap. XXI, nn. 1-4; F. Wernz, *Ius Decretalium* (6 vols., Romae 1898-1914; Vol. II, 3. ed., Prati, 1915), II, 84.

[4] J. Rossi, *De Paroecia* (Romae: Pustet, 1923), p. 3.

[5] *Ibidem*, pp. 8-9; L. Ferraris, *Prompta Bibliotheca Canonica, Iuridica, Moralis, Theologica necnon Ascetica, Polemica, Rubristica, Historica* 9 vols. Romae, 1885-1899) s.v. *Parochia*, n. 7; St. Ignatius, *Epistola ad Smyrnaeos*, cap. 8, n. 2—Migne, *Patrologiae Cursus Completus, Series Graeca* (161 vols., Parisiis, 1857-1866), V, 71 (hereafter cited *MPG*).

[6] *Canones Apostolorum*, can. 39 — Funk, *Didascalia et Constitutiones Apostolorum* (2 vols., Paderbornae, 1905), I, 577.

[7] Cf. Poulet — Raemers, *A History of the Catholic Church* (2 vols., translated from the 4. French edition, London: B. Herder Book Co., 1935-1936; reprint, 1948) I, 176; *Codex Theodosianus* (edd. P. Kruger et Th. Mommsen, Berolini: Apud Weidmannos, 1905), (16,10) 12.

had to be erected and priests given duties that formerly devolved on the bishop alone. No longer could the Church be established solely in urban areas. Since the cathedral churches proved insufficient, rural oratories arose in the West and in the East.[8] Many of these became known as *ecclesiae maiores* or *baptismales,* and were the true forerunners of parishes.[9]

In contradistinction to the priests who had had only special delegation for individual acts, the priests of the *ecclesiae maiores* had the special distinction of acting in their own name, though with restricted rights.[10] For example, from the fifth century onward the priest of an *ecclesia maior* had the right to administer solemn baptism and to celebrate mass on Sundays and holy days for the people.[11] Coronata points out that these baptismal churches began, more and more, to assume the aspect of parochial institutes in the fifth and sixth centuries.[12] However, the priest was not an irremovable pastor; he was not only fully subject to but also completely dependent on the bishop in the exercise of his pastoral work.

From the middle of the fifth century the unity of the old dioceses began to break up. Country churches, which as property had been subject to the supervisory restrictions of the dioceses, became financially self-sufficient. So, too, did the newly founded

[8] Council of Sardica (343) — J. Mansi, *Sacrorum Conciliorum Nova et Amplissima Collectio* (53 vols. in 60, Vols. 1-31, Florentiae, Venetiis, Parisiis, 1759-1798: Vols. 31b53, Parisiis, Lepizig, Arnhem, 1901-1927), III, 10 (hereafter cited Mansi); Council of Chalcedon (451) — Mansi, VIII, 397; Cf. Bastnagel, *The Appointment of Parochial Adjutants and Assistants,* The Catholic University of America Canon Law Studies, n. 58 (Washington, D. C.: The Catholic University of America, 1930), p.8.

[9] P. Hinschius, *Das Kirchenrecht der Katholiken und Protestanten in Deutschland* (6 vols., Berlin, 1869-1897) II, 263.

[10] J. Devoti, *Institutionum Canonicarum Libri IV* (4 vols., Leodii, 1860), Lib. I, Tit. III, Sect. X; Mansi, III, 1930.

[11] Roman Synod of 402, can. 7 — Mansi, III, 1137; Waldron, *The Minister of Baptism,* The Catholic University of America Canon Law Studies, n. 170 (Washington, D. C.: The Catholic University of America Press, 1942), p. 30.

[12] *Institutiones Iuris Canonici* (2. ed., 5 vols., Taurini: Marietti, 1939-1947), I, n. 305.

private churches and the baptismal churches.[13] Yet an individual division of the country churches from the diocese was not known in Italy at least through the time of the Lombards.[14]

In Lower Saxony and in Scandinavia the progress of the missions made a partition of the parishes necessary. Private churches began to acquire, bit by bit, the restricted rights of baptismal churches, such as the holding of Sunday services, the granting of burial, the bestowing of a blessing on marriages, and eventually the conferring of baptism. Thus, around the ninth century, there existed many churches with limited parish rights within the old extensive parishes.[15]

In the cities, however, still more time was to elapse before parish churches as such were founded. Dependence on the cathedral church continued, with the priests carrying on their duties in the name of the bishop. But with the passage of time the cathedral church of the bishop was no longer capable of offering a full parochial care. According to Bouix (1808-1870), it was about the year 1000 that cities and towns were finally divided into parochial districts, with the exception only of Rome and Alexandria, these two great centers having long before instituted a similar procedure.[16]

Modern authorities, however, disagree with this date. Dr. Heinrich Schaefer, after research, states that in many of the urban areas city parishes existed as early as the ninth century. To prove his assertion he specifically lists the names of a few.[17] It can also be shown that as early as the ninth century many parish churches, administrated by collegiate chapters which had acquired rights of a parochial nature, also appeared in the cities.[18] These collegiate churches in the episcopal cities took care of the parish services, while

[13] Feine, *Kirchliche Rechtsgeschichtes Die katholische Kirche* (Weimar: Hermann Bohlaus Nachfolger, 1950), p. 116 (hereafter cited Feine).

[14] Feine, p. 117.

[15] Feine, p. 159,

[16] D. Bouix, *Tractatus de Parocho* (3. ed., Parisiis, 1880), I, 1.

[17] *Pfarrkirche und Stift im Deutschen Mittelalter, Kirchenrechtliche Abhandlugen,* hrsg. von U. Stutz, 3. Heft (Stuttgart, 1903) pp. 23-28.

[18] Kelly, *The Functions Reserved to Pastors,* The Catholic University of America Canon Law Studies, n. 250 (Washington, D. C.: The Catholic University of America Press, 1947) p. 8; Feine, p. 166.

the cathedral church with its chapter served the entire diocese. With the passage of time, the cathedral and collegiate churches won a distinct corporate character.[19]

In summary, it may be said that rural parishes began in the fourth or fifth century, and city parishes in the ninth. But it is logical to assume that even after these dates some time must have elapsed before the pastor acquired a determined status.

That in itself can serve as an explanation for the non-existence of real registers in the earliest days of the Church, and for the scarcity of source material in this matter up to the middle ages. There were, however, indications of what was to come.

Article II: The Diptychs

The earliest indication worthy of note for the parish census and the parochial spiritual status register is to be found in the diptychs. The diptych, as the name suggests, was a kind of note book, generally made of wood, ivory, bone, or metal, and formed through the union of two tablets, placed one upon the other and united by means of rings or a hinge.[20] Ordinarily its inner surfaces had a raised frame covered with wax, upon which the characters were scratched. From as far back as the sixth century B. C., the diptychs had served as copy books. Now, in the early Christian ages it was customary to write on the diptychs the names of those, living or dead, who were considered as members of the church.

a) Diptychs of the living

It was in the "diptychs of the living" that can be recognized in barest outline the parochial spiritual status register of today.[21] Included in this list were the names of the pope, of the bishop, of illustrious persons, either lay or ecclesiastical, of the benefactors of the church, and of those who offered the Holy Sacrifice therein.[22]

19 Feine, p. 167.

20 Cabrol — Leclercq — Marrou, "Diptychon," *Dictionnaire d' Archèologie Chrétienne et de Liturgie* (Paris, 1907) Vol. IV, Part I, 1040, d.

21 O'Rourke, p. 25.

22 J. Cavalieri, *Opera Omnia Liturgia* (5 vols., Venetiis, 1758) V, 67 (hereafter cited Cavalieri).

The use of these diptychs is vouched for in the writings of St. Cyprian (210-258) in the third century.[23] In *Epistle LXVI* Cyprian spoke of "another being substituted" in the diptychs for the infamous Marcian, who had been excommunicated because of his close association with Novatian.[24] This readily implies that the name of Marcian had been striken from the list of those who were in good standing, for it was the then prevailing custom to use the diptychs as a proof of orthodoxy.

That such a development had taken place is evident in the writing of St. Cyril of Jerusalem (313-386), especially in the *Procatechesis,* when he spoke of the sincerity of those in the church:

> Nevertheless, you have entered, you have been admitted, and your name has been inscribed. Do you see the ideal of the church, an ideal worthy of veneration? Do you see the order and discipline? The lessons of Scripture, the presence of canonical persons (or those inscribed on the ecclesiastical registers), the order and succession of teaching? May you be moved by the reverence of this place and learn from those things which you behold.[25]

The diptychs of the living, of which alone there is question here, admitted only the names of persons in communion with the church.[26] The names of heretics and of the excommunicated were never inserted. Exclusion from these lists was considered a grave eccælesiastical penalty. The fact that the content of the diptychs was read aloud from the altar or ambo by the priest or deacon as a testimony of orthodoxy brought the status of such people before the attention of the whole community. In connection with this read-

[23] St. Cyprianus, *Epist. LX* — J. Migne, *Patrologiae Cursus Completus, Series Latina* (221 vols., Parisiis, 1844-1855), IV, 362 (hereafter cited *MPL*); *Epist. LXII* — *Corpus Scriptorum Ecclesiasticorum Latinorum* (71 vols. [incomplete], Vindobonae, 1866) III, part II, 701 (hereafter cited *CSEL.*

[24] *MPL,* IV, 367; cf. also *Epist. LXVIII* — *CSEL,* Vol. III, part II, 745.

[25] *Procatechesis,* I, 4 — *MPG,* XXXIII, 339.

[26] Cavalieri, V, 67.

ing, it is interesting to note that, though the time and manner varied in different localities, all held it in high honor.[27]

In most places the reading was begun at mass time, with the reader halting for the most solemn parts of the sacrifice. The Syro-Byzantine liturgies placed it between the Kiss of Peace and the Preface.[28] In the liturgy of St. Basil (330-379), so it is pointed out, "the deacon incenses the holy table in its entirety, and then at his discretion runs quickly over the diptychs of the living and the dead."[29]

Naturally, as the numbers of the faithful grew, it was necessary to mention explicitly only the more illustrious, and to advert to the rest in general commemoration. Time did not permit the doing of it otherwise. Bona (1609-1674) stated that there was need of a month or a year at the services for the complete reading of the names of all parishioners.[30] Conversely one may argue that, since it was possible at one time in a given service to read all the names of the faithful in a community, these lists must have existed from a very early period.

Other Fathers of the Church also furnish testimony regarding the use of the diptychs. The writings of St. John Chrysostom (344-407) bear witness to their use as do the writings of St. Jerome (344-420),[31]

b) Diptychs of the baptized, married, deceased, etc.

It should not be thought that the diptychs were limited to what is known as the diptych of the living. There were diptychs of the baptized, of the married, of the dead, and of those who made offerings for the Mass, each with its own peculiar history and purpose.[32] These will be treated briefly in turn.

[27] Parsch — Eckhoff, *The Liturgy of the Mass* (St. Louis and London: B. Herder Book Co., 1942), p. 225.

[28] Duchesne — McClure, *Christian Worship* (London, 1903), p. 84 (hereafter cited Duchesne-McClure).

[29] *Enciclopedia Universal Illustrada* (Barcelona: Hyon de J. Espasa, 1903-) XVIII, 1397.

[30] Bona, *Rerum Liturgicarum Libri Duo* (Taurini, 1747-1753, Lib. II, Cap. XII, p. 394 (hereafter cited Bona).

[31] *Enciclopedia Universal Illustrada, loc. cit.*

[32] Bona, Lib. II, cap. XII, p. 390.

According to O'Rourke the diptych of the baptized was simply a list of the newly baptized and, unlike the diptychs of the living and the dead, was never meant to be read publicly. Since it was to be kept in the bishop's house, he concluded that it was for the bishop's private use.[33] Duchesne (1843-1922), however, feels otherwise. He states (with an abundance of historical evidence) that this list was ordinarily read in the commemoration of the Mass at Easter and Pentecost. Moreover, he would include among the diptychs of the baptized a list of the candidates for baptism. As explained these latter names were publicly announced on the days of "scrutiny" in order to obtain any information the faithful may have had concerning the fitness of the aspirants to baptism.[34]

The diptych of the married was also used in the early days of the Church merely for the implementation of a praiseworthy custom. By means of this diptych it was possible to make a special memento in the Mass of the couples listed therein on the 30th day following their wedding and again each year on the anniversary of the marriage ceremony itself.[35] So too was the diptych of the deceased kept for a spiritual purpose—that of commemorating the faithful departed in the sacrifice of the Mass and other liturgical functions.

The list of those who made offerings at Mass-time, on the other-hand, was kept to stimulate the faithful to greater generosity and to publicly thank those who had contributed. It is interesting to note that when Innocent I (401-417) was called upon to determine whether the offerings and the names of the donors were to be read before or after the Mass prayers, he replied in favor of the latter.[36] The same Pope, however, soon curtailed the publication of this list because of the possible scandal it involved.

It is to be noted that none of the diptychs had as their main purpose the matter of proof with the exception of the "diptych of the living" in regard to orthodoxy. Moreover, none of these records were to last, for the establishment of Christianity in the Empire

33 O'Rourke, p. 21.

34 Duchesne-McClure, p. 180.

35 Bona, Lib. II, cap. XII, p. 394.

36 Labbeus—Cossartius, *Sacrosancta Consilia* (17 vols. in 18, Lutetiate Parisiorum, 1671-1672), II, 1246.

made the diptychs dwindle in importance until they were "lost in the course of time: when Christianity became the state religion the civil registers began to take their place."[37] After the fifth century, virtually no trace of them survives.[38]

ARTICLE III: OTHER REFERENCES TO PARISH LISTS

Perhaps the last refence to "parish" lists in this period occurred in the *Historia Ecclesiastica* of Evagrius (536-600), who wrote: "Such, then, was the situation of the churchs throughout the world down to the reign of Anastasius (491-518), whom some, treating him as an enemy to the Synod at Chalcedon, erased from the sacred diptychs or parish lists."[39] It has previously been seen that these lists began with the names of the pope, of the bishop, and of other illustrious persons both ecclesastical and lay. Evidently Emperor Anastasius came under the latter heading. But because of his unbecoming conduct, his name was stricken from the diptych and omitted in the commoration of the Mass. The custom of including mention of worthy lay dignitaries in the Mass, however, continued to the sixteenth century, when so many of the temporal rulers broke away from the Church.[40]

Surely, then, a kind of church register did exist. In summarizing this period one may say that the keeping of parish lists seems to have been a practice that grew out of circumstances and was accepted by all as a matter of course, but one concerning which no direct legislation can be found.

It appears that the first enacted legislation on the subject of the census and the parochial spiritual status register appeared in a synod of the year 880. According to Cavigioli this was published

[37] Saegmüller, "Die Entstehung und Entwicklung der Kirchenbücher im Katholischen Deutchland bis zur Mitte der 18. Jahrhunderts," *Theologische Quartalschrift* (*TQS*), LXXXI (1889), 216.

[38] Mabillon, *Acta Sanctorum Ordinis S. Benedicti in Classes Saeculorum Distributa* (9 vols., Venetiis, 1783), Praefatio ad V Saeculum, VII, n. 97, p. 416.

[39] Lib. III, cap. 34, *MPG,* LXXXVI bis, 2674.

[40] Semeria-Berry, *The Eucharistic Liturgy in the Roman Rite* (Ratisbon: Pustet & Co., 1911), p. 143.

for the first time in the *Spicilegium Casinense* (t. I, 1893, pg.377). There the prescription is found, "let every priest have in writing the individual names of his people."[41] While the object of this ruling certainly could not be called a parochial spiritual status register as we know it today, it was a worthy indication of what was to come. Many more centuries, however, were to elapse before the true notion of this register would be fully developed.

[41] Cavigioli, *Manuale di diritto canonico* (3. ed., Torino, Società Editrice Internazionale, 1946), p. 314, footnote.

CHAPTER III

DEVELOPMENT IN THE MIDDLE AGES

ARTICLE I: CORPUS IURIS CANONICI

A survey of the *Corpus Iuris Canonici* gives no direct evidence of a parochial spiritual status register or of the parish census, but in it one finds evidence of an indirect character. In it one can see the growing tendency to make pastors more cognizant of what the *cura animarum* involved. From the *Decretum Gratiani* and the *Liber Sextus* as well as from the interpretation of the decretalists it is clear that the *cura animarum* included more than just a mere administration of the sacraments. The spiritual jurisdiction of the parish priest included the notions of rule and government, of viligance and correction, and of the maintenance of good order among the subjects committed to his care.[1]

Yet, particular stress was placed on the yearly Communion and confession. As an instance one may look to Gratian (✠ca. 1157). Summarizing a decree attributed by him to Pope Fabian (236-350), he wrote; "All of the faithful are to receive Communion three times a year."[2] And again; "Those who purposely neglect to communicate these three times a year: Christmas, Easter, and Pentecost, are not to be regarded as Catholics."[3] Finally in a canon drawn from the I Council of Toledo, held in the year 400 during the reign of Pope St. Anastasius I (399-401), Gratian quotes that "those are to be rebuked who disregard Communion."

In connection with this text is found a *casus* worthy of note. The glossator made it clear that if people had mortal sin on their souls they were first to do penance before receiving, and refusing to

[1] *Glossa ordinaria* s. v. *Praecepimus,* c. 5, C. XXI, q. 2; c. 6, *de praebendis et dignitatibus,* III, 4, in VI°; Henricus de Segusio, *In Quinque Decreatium Commentaria* (vols. in 3, Venetiis, 1581), Lib. V. tit. 38 *de poenitentiis et remissionibus,* cap. XI, n. 12.

[2] C. 16, D. II, *de cons.*

[3] Taken by Gratian from the 18th canon of the Council of Agde (506) —c. 19, D. II, *de cons.*

do penance they were to be subject to excommunication.[4] Abstention from Communion was not simply a matter of one's own choice.[5]

But, since many of the faithful had begun to disregard these laws dealing with confession and Communion, the IV General Council of the Lateran (1215) deemed it necessary to command all the faithful, upon obtaining the use of reason, to confess to their *own* parish priest at least once a year and to receive Communion at Easter time. Failure to fulfill this law would result in their being barred from entering a church during life and in their being deprived of Christian burial in death.[6]

Gregory IX (1227-1241), realizing the great import of this canon, incorporated it in its entirety in his Decretals (1234) with the accompanying rubic: "Famosum est et multum allegabile, et hoc dicit: Quilibet doli capax tenetur saltem semel in anno confiteri proprio sacerdoti, vel de eius licentia alteri, et Eucharistiae sacramentum ad minus in Pascha recipere."[7] In order to facilitate the enforcement of such a law, it is evident that a record needed to be kept by pastors of those who made their annual confession and Easter Communion. Thus is this law the motivating cause behind the introduction of much legislation concerning parochial registers.

Article II: Legislation On Registers In Later Councils And Synods

There can be no doubt, however, that parish registers were enjoined and used only locally before the Council of Trent.[8] What is to be said in the following deals solely with particular law as affecting widely scattered areas and different nationalities with divergent customs and needs. Thus, to believe that generally one

[4] C. 20, D. II, *de cons.*

[5] C. 18, D. II, *de cons.*

[6] IV General Council of the Lateran (1215), canon 21—Mansi, XXII, 1007.

[7] *Corpus Iuris Canonici,* Pars. II, *Decretalium Collectiones* (Editio Lipsiensis II, post Aemilii Ludovici Richteri curas . . . instruxit Aemilius Friedberg, Lipsiae, 1881), c. 12, X, *de poenitentiis et remissionibus,* V, 38.

[8] Jedin, "Konzil von Trient und Kirchenmatrikeln," *Zeitschrift der Savigny—Stiftung* (*ZSS*), Kanonistische Abteilung (Weimar; Verlag Hermann Böhlaus Nachfolger, 1911-), XXXII (1943), 419-494.

council influenced the next would be false. At times exceptions to this must be made, as when two councils were held in the same city or in adjacent localities. Nevertheless, in viewing the decisions of various provincial councils and synods, one sees a development by external addition, as it were, or better still, an evolution that was one day to reach fruition in the universal law as stated in the *Roman Ritual* of Paul V (1614). From his time forward the development moved at a rapid pace.

About fifty years after the Decretals of Gregory IX, in 1286 to be exact, the Council of Beziers enacted two important laws, the one concerning excommunication; the other, confession. These were important, for they placed on the rectors of parishes the obligation of recording such events. Canon ten reads: "We rule that each rector of a church, and any one taking his place, is to keep individual records in which he is to write all the names of those who are excommunicated from his own parish. . ."[9] "Likewise we state that each parish priest should warn his parishioners that they are to confess all their sins to him at least once a year; and the names of those so confessing are to be recorded in writing, that they may be given Communion at Eastertide."[10] Nothing is said of the type of book to be used, or where it was to be kept.

A council held at Salamanca in 1335 extended the notion of parish records, ruling that they were to be shown to the bishop upon his visitation. In chapter 16, which treats of penance and the remission of sins, reference is made to a listing of all parishioners:

> We prescribe that pastors who are held to render an account to the bishop concerning the care of souls, in virtue of holy obedience and under the pain of excommunication shall write in one book the names of all their parishioners, so that at least at the time of visitation they are able to point out those who are unwilling to receive the sacraments, whereupon the bishop himself may punish them more severly.[11]

[9] Hardouin, *Acta Conciliorum et Epistolae Decretales ac Constitutiones Summorum Pontificum* (12 vols., Parisiis, 1714-1715), VII, 952-953 (hereafter cited Hardouin); Mansi, XXIV, 629.

[10] Can. 13 — Hardouin, VII, 954; Mansi, XXIV, 631.

[11] Hardouin, VII, 1974; Mansi XXV, 1057.

Four years later a provincial council was convoked at Toledo. There the idea of an annual inscription of names was introduced. Moreover, a ruling concerning those names which were to be included was given. It was decreed that all, once they had reached the use of reason, were to be inscribed in the record by the church rectors and their vicars under pain of excommunication. This Council was concerned with the obligation of confession and Communion and the question of sin. Hence the inscription of the names of anyone not having the use of reason was completely waived.[12]

Over a century later, in 1454, a diocesan synod, convoked in Pomerania, decreed, as had the Council of Beziers, that pastors in their own diocese diligently keep a book recording the names of those who had contracted excommunication, extending it, however, to include those under penalty and interdict, and giving as the purpose for such a book that, if for any reason the pastor should leave the parish, his successor would immediately know those under censure.[13]

An interesting point of evolution in parish lists, that of using the alphabetical order, was legislated by the Bishop of Speyer in 1474, when speaking of a listing of all the parishioners in each parish of his diocese.[14] Though this was probably the custom long before, the ruling as here enacted was the first explicit legislation on the point. Shortly after, in 1498, Cardinal Francisco Ximenes de Cisneros (1436-1517), then the Archbishop of Toledo, in the Synod of Talavera, Spain, decreed in the sixteenth constitution that each pastor was to make a list of all his parishioners according to families. In it he was to note those who had not confessed or communicated up to the 20th day after Easter.[15]

[12] Can. V. — Hardouin, VII, 1638; Mansi, XXV, 1146.

[13] *Concilia Germaniae,* Joannis Mauritii sumptu, Joannes Fridericus Schannat collegit et P. Josephus Hartzheim auxit et continuavit (11 vols., Coloniae Augustae Agrippinensium: Typo viduae Joan. Wilhelmi Krakamp, et haeredum Christiani Simonis, Bibliopolarum, 1759-1790), V, 935.

[14] H. Jedin, "La origine dei registri parrocchiali e il Concilio di Trento," found in the review *Il Concilio di Trento* (Pubblicazione Trimestrale a cura del Comitato per il IV Centenario del Concilio Tridentino — Curia Arcivescovile — Trento), Roma, Anno II, n. 4, Ottobre 1943, p. 323 (hereafter cited "La origine dei registri parrocchiali").

[15] Jedin, "Konzil von Trient und Kerchenmatrikeln," *ZSS,* Kan. Abtlg., XXXII (1943), 447.

In 1512, the Council of Seville treated the pastor's obligation to keep a catalogue of those who had failed to confess and also to receive the Eucharist, as well as those who had been excommunicated because of public sins. This catalogue, signed by the pastor, was to be sent to the *Provisores* each year before Low Sunday, and to be used in church for the denouncement of those who had incurred the sentence of excommunication.[16]

Finally, what appears to be the last legislation of the pre-Tridentine period on the parochial spiritual status register is found in a synod convoked in Augsburg by Cardinal Otto Truchsess of Waldburg (1514-1573) in 1548. In it one finds the beginnings of a scientific treatment of the parish records and an expansion of the notion of the *liber*:

> All pastors or all priests to whom has been given the care of souls should keep four books in their churches, the first containing the names of the baptized, the second, of those who confessed and communicated at the time stated by the Church, the third, of those who contracted marriage in the Church, and the fourth containing, along with a notation of the day and the year, the names of the deceased who have been given ecclesiastical burial. This diligence is useful in many ways, but especially since it makes more evident to the pastor the condition of souls.[17]

While the contents of the first and third mentioned books are generally included in our present register, the closest resemblance is is with the second book. It is confession, the spiritual regeneration of the soul, and Communion, the nourishment of the soul, that in the main determines the status of souls.

Nevertheless it is held, and with good reason, that the parochial spiritual status register is a development, even though indirectly, of more than those books which listed the faithful who had fulfilled their obligations of annual confession and Easter Communion, and of those who were in communion with the Church itself, and hence were not excommunicated.[18]

16 Mansi, XXXII, 588.

17 Cap. VIII — Mansi, XXXII, 1302.

18 Jedin, "art. cit.," *ibid.*, p. 478.

In contemplating this period of history one can find, not a real parochial spiritual status register, but rather individual registers of baptisms, marriages, and deaths, as well as of the acts whereby parishioners fulfilled their yearly duties. Priests of those centuries used such records in trying to be real shepherds of souls, observing carefully the manner in which the faithful were progressing towards God. In doing so they drew upon *all* the registers, that they might obtain a *complete* picture of the status of the souls under their care.

It was only natural that baptismal records were the first to be kept. Through baptism the pagan became incorporated into the Mystical Body of Christ. Through it was one to be numbered among the elect and allowed to receive the spiritual nourishment of the other sacraments. Naturally enough marriage records also were kept, besides the records of confirmation, confession, and the fulfillment of the Easter duty.

To mention a few of the earlier records still in existence at this time does not seem amiss: in France, one may see the parish books of Givry started in 1335, listing marriages and deaths, and those of Loire (1469) listing baptisms and marriages; in Italy the church of San Frediano in Lucca proudly displays its baptismal register begun in 1477. In Germany may be found the diocesan statutes (1435) of the Bishop of Constance requiring baptismal and marriage registers in all parishes. The same is true in the Low Countries (The Netherlands) in regard to the diocesan statutes of Tournai (1481) which demanded a baptismal register. There is evidence that by the beginning of the sixteenth century Spain, Portugal, England, and Scotland had enacted similar legislation.[19]

Though such records as those of baptism and marriage exist up to our day as separate entities, they did play a part in the formation of the parochial spiritual status register. While separate in one sense, as records for proof, they are interrelated in the *cura animarum*, for the parochial spiritual status register summarizes their contents before adding additional information relative to the state of souls.

Thus far has been traced the parochial spiritual status register from its vague beginnings, as found in the diptychs, through its de-

[19] *Ibid*, pp. 419-494.

velopment in various councils, synods, and decrees. Such notions as to who were to be included, who were obliged to make these lists, how were they to be made, and what was to be done with them when once they were duly compiled, all received treatment according as they became manifest in history. But it was only after the Council of Trent that a clear notion of the parish census became incorporated in laws that sought to promote the further development of the parochial spiritual status register.

CHAPTER IV

THE COUNCIL OF TRENT AND ITS INFLUENCE

Article I: The Council Of Trent

Though the Council of Trent (1545-1563) did not make any explicit mention of the parochial spiritual status register, it did evidence great concern over the *cura animarum* as exercised by pastors. Reminding them of their position as shepherds of souls, it admonished and exhorted all who had the care of souls to know and watch over the flock.[1] They were not to be as hirelings, ready to desert in time of distress, but were to follow the example of the divine Savior, who at the end of his mortal life was able to say: "Those whom Thou gavest me have I kept; and none of them is lost, but the son of perdition."[2] By prayer and labor, by word and example, He had showed them the way to eternal happiness. He had understood and taught that the better one knows his parish, the wiser and more efficient direction will he be able to give his parishioners. "The good shepherd knows his sheep."[3]

Surely, then, this exhortation of the Council of Trent embraced practices that had already developed in individual dioceses and parishes throughout the world: that of taking parish censuses and keeping records on the condition of souls. Hubert Jedin pointed to this when he wrote: "The Council of Trent introduced nothing new; it merely accepted, strengthened, and universalized the statutes and usages of various regions."[4] Perhaps the very reason for the lack of any explicit reference by the Council to these parochial practices was the fact that it was all too evident that the census and its recording (two of the main aids by which one with care of souls might fulfill the given directives) were already being used.

1 Conc. Trident., sess XXIII, de ref., c. 1 — Schroeder, *Council of Trent,* p. 146.

2 John, XVII; 12.

3 John, X: 14

4 *La origine dei registri parrocchiali,* p. 1.

Be that as it may, the Council in the 24th session, held under Pope Pius IV in 1563, did make explicit reference to baptismal and marriage registers. The reasons are clear. At that time the impediment of spiritual relationship was rather extensive. It arose between the sponsors and the baptized, between the sponsors and the mother and the father of the baptized, as well as between the one baptizing and the one baptized, and between the one baptizing and the mother and the father of the one baptized. In order to avoid confusion and to safeguard future marriages, the Council ruled that the parish priest faithfully record in the baptismal book the names of all the afore-mentioned.[5]

Marriage books, too, were to be kept and preserved. They were to include the names of the newly married and of the witnesses, together with a notation of the day and the place of the marriage.[6] Thus were legislated measures, very simple, yet very important, for the matter of proof, something which the ancient Canon Law had failed to provide.

Article II: Particular Legislation

The tremendous influence that the Council of Trent exerted in its desire to reestablish in the clergy a real zeal for knowing and helping souls was evident, almost at once, throughout the world. Particular councils and synods for all Christendom began to legislate on the obligations of parish priests. There arose a sense of awareness of the gravity of the duties incumbent upon those having the care of souls, along with a realization that to minister properly to their people called for an intimate knowledge of them. In the very year following the Council of Trent, 1564, the Church of Bergamo in a Synod made specific mention of the *Liber status animarum* as one of the books to be kept by all pastors.[7] But it was in Milan that one could find a most thorough treatment of the question. There, under the guidance of St. Charles Borromeo (1538-1584), a series of Provincial Councils showed a remarkable interest in the duties incumbent upon the parish priest, and especially

[5] Schroeder, *Council of Trent,* p. 186.

[6] Ibid., p. 186.

[7] *La origine dei registri parrocchiali,* p. 1.

in his obligation to keep parish registers. When one realizes the condition of the Church at that period, it is not at all surprising to to see this unusual interest.

The I Provincial Council, in 1565, in referring to the bishop's obligation to know his flock, began by quoting the very beautiful passage of Scripture found in the 34th chapter of Ezechiel, foretelling the coming of Christ as the true pastor, who would gather together his flock from all parts of the earth and preserve it forever. In like manner was the bishop to learn of the conditions in his diocese and, if need be, make paternal corrections. To accomplish this required a careful selection of those clerics who were to "investigate in the parishes whether the faithful walked in the way of the Lord," and then relay to the bishop the result of their survey.

The pastors for their part, were to keep on hand a book containing the names and surnames of all in the parish, along with a record of their sex, age, and status. In it also were to be recorded recent births and deaths, as well as the names of those entering and leaving the parish. Evidently it was desired that the register be kept up to date. In turn, the bishop, on his visitation, was to examine the book carefully.[8] Moreover, the bishop was to call in all the pastors on the Ember days, and diligently inquire of them the state of the souls in their respective parishes, instilling in these clerics a spirit of diligence and viligance.[9]

The II Provincial Council, held four years later, required two other books, one listing those who had received Extreme Unction, the other those who had received the Paschal Communion. The latter precept was ordinarily to be fulfilled in one's proper parish. For acknowledging a parish as one's own, a person either had to be a resident in it for at least six months, or had at least to have the intention of making the parish his place of domicile. If neither condition was verified, a written permission of one's proper bishop or pastor was necessary to fulfill the Paschal obligation, in which case

[8] *Acta Ecclesiae Mediolanensis,* a Sancto Carolo Cardinali S. Praxedis Archiep. condita, Frederici Cardinalis Borromaei Archiepisopi Mediolani jussu collecta et edita (2 vols., Lugduni; Ex Officina Anissoniana et Joan. Posuel, 1682-1683), Tom. I, Pars I, p. 20 (hereafter cited *AEM*).

[9] *AEM,* Tom. I, Pars I, p. 21.

the pastor of the parish wherein the precept had been fulfilled was to record the name, surname, and domicile of the *peregrini or advenae.*[10]

The III Provincial Council (1573) added that the pastor was not to make known any information contained in the parish books without the permission of the bishop. Even after the bishop's permission had been obtained by the pastor, the latter was not to furnish the information in writing, unless a person had inquired regarding some factor in relation to his own birth or with reference to his age.[11]

Between the III and IV Provincial Councils, St. Charles Borromeo, under whom all these councils were held, issued a most detailed and complete instruction (1574) on the parochial spiritual status register. He began by reiterating the commands of the councils that each pastor should make a catalogue of all the souls within the limits of his parish. In as much as many had neglected to do as he had ordered, thus giving rise to many inconveniences and even making it impossible to know who had been confirmed, who had made their Easter duty, and who had reached the required age for the reception of the other sacraments, he warned all pastors that, putting aside all excuses, they were to send the record to him according to the method indicated, keeping one copy for themselves. This obligation was to be fulfilled between the feast of St. Martin and Ash Wednesday. Failure would result in the payment of a fine which when discharged would become applicable to the holy places.

He did permit pastors, however, to use the same record for the following two or three years, provided they made provisions for the entering of any changes occurring within the family status during that time. a record of which was to be sent in each year. For this purpose a day-book was to be kept, and in it the following notations were to be made: the names of the new-born in a family, of the new parishioners, of the deceased, of those who had moved away, also of those who within the year had received Communion or Confirmation, whether in the parish or elsewhere, as also of those who had become ten years of age within the year. This information was then to be arranged in alphabetical order and written in the parochial spiritual status register. Mention also was to be made of the village

[10] *AEM,* Tom. I, Pars I, p. 53.

[11] *AEM,* Tom. I, Pars I, p. 80.

or town wherein the parishioners dwelt or, in the event of a large and densely populated city, of the district. When more than one family lived in the same house, each family was to be inscribed under a separate family heading. However, the address as given was to point to the place where the person actually dwelt, irrespective of the residence of the father.

In order to keep the records in a more orderly and uniform manner, he ordered a common set of symbols be used, for example, "Co." for Communion, "Ch." for Confirmation, "✠" for those who had departed from this life, and an "X" for those who had reached 10 years of age. The latter mark was to remind the pastor that he should see that the person in question went to confession and was given a written testimony to that effect as well as to make it clear that he was eligible for the reception of the Sacrament of Confirmation. When these sacraments had been received, the X was to be removed. St. Charles Borromeo further added that the pastor was very frequently to check this list and to keep it up-to-date by means of a house to house visitation.

No one was to be shown this register except the bishop. Included in it were to be such factors as touched on the age, sex, occupation and religious profession of the respective individuals, the single or married state, and their relationship to the head of the family. The pastor could include additional useful information if he so desired. Even the adoption of a different method in the recording, if such an adaptation proved more serviceable, stood fully commended and approved. Thus did the saintly and practical Archbishop of Milan conclude his instruction.[12]

Two years later the IV Provincial Council (1576) was convoked at Milan. Of interest was its regulation that priest confessors, even regulars, beside recording the names of the penitents at Eastertime, give to the penitent a written testimonial signed and stamped with the seal of the church, attesting the fact of his confession. Thus it could be made evident to the pastor at Paschal time, and in time of sickness to the doctor, that one's obligation had been fulfilled. Lest any kind of fraud intervene, the names and surnames of those who had confessed at Easter time were not only not to be withheld,

[12] *AEM,* Tom. I, Pars IV, p. 685.

but were to be shown promptly to the bishop upon request, and handed over to him in a book. He was to determine the form in which this testimony was to appear and, when possible, have blank copies printed for and distributed to each confessor.[13]

Under the title, *"Quae pertinent ad Extremam Unctionem"* in the same Council, it was made incumbent on pastors to report monthly to the rural dean the names of those who had died during that time, and to render a statement about the care given to them during their sickness as well as regarding the service rendered after their death.[14] The record of these acts was to be preserved by the pastor in an archive or in the sacristy, and was to be available to the bishop at the time of his visitation.[15]

During these years of Provincial Councils, 11 diocesan synods were also convoked in Milan. The 5th held in the year 1578, included a table of offenses which if committed called for the imposing of a money fine. One of the items specifically mentioned was the parochial spiritual status register. Failure to have a register, to keep it up to date, or failure to send a copy to the bishop at the required time, made one subject to the penalty.[16] At that time it was also determined, but by the Apostolic Visitator, that it was the pastor upon whom the duty of keeping the parochial spiritual status register in the prescribed form was incumbent.[17]

The two later Provincial Councils of Milan, held in 1579 and 1582, add nothing to what has already been said. In the meantime, however, legislation, though also particular, was being enacted in other dioceses throughout the world on the role of the parochial spiritual status register in the parochial care of souls. For example, the Provincial Council of Salzburg, in 1569, ordered the keeping of three books: the first was to contain the names of all the faithful of either sex, giving also their age and condition of life; the second, the names of the deceased; and the third, a day book, to provide new

13 *AEM*, Tom. I, Pars II, p. 114.
14 *AEM*, Tom. I, Pars II, p. 114.
15 *AEM*, Tom. I, Pars III, p. 142.
16 *AEM*, Tom. II, Pars IV, p. 890.
17 *AEM*, Tom. I, Pars III, p. 387.

material for the first. Both old and new parishioners were to be catalogued and a record of their spiritual estate and of their reception of the sacraments was to be included.[18]

In 1581, the Provincial Council of Rouen, apparently influenced by the decrees of the Synod of Augsburg (1548), convoked under Cardinal Truchsess of Waldburg, demanded in practically the same words the same four books.[19] The second book, containing the names of those who had made their Easter confession and Communion, involved a particularly noteworthy connotation which has already been explained elsewhere.[20]

The Provincial Council of Bordeaux, held two years later, enacted similar regulations,[21] as did the Provincial Council of Cambrai (1586).[22] In addition, this legislative body demanded that an archive be used for the preservation of the parochial records, if the church was a collegiate one; if a parish church, then the sacristan was to care for the books. The privilege of inspection, moreover, pertained solely to the pastor and to the parties to whom it could be of a rightful special interest.[23] Although the foregoing regulations of Cambrai directly applied to the baptismal and marriage registers, they did not abstract from the book in which the names of the shriven and the communicants were entered.

Though it did not specifically mention the *"liber status animarum"* by name, the Provincial Council of Ratisbon (1588) likewise desired that pastors keep a book containing family names, the names of the individual members thereof, the record of their age and relationship, mention of whether they had confessed and communicated, and whether they had received confirmation and entered marriage. A notation, by way of symbols, was to be made if they had changed parishes or had died.[24]

At Toulouse, a Provincial Council in 1590, while not requiring a register, did urge the pastor to inquire of, and observe, the cus-

18 *Concilia Germaniae,* VII, 292.

19 Hardouin, X, 1237.

20 *Supra,* p. 24.

21 Hardouin, X, 1355.

22 *Concilia Germaniae,* VII, 1004, 1005, 1009.

23 *Concilia Germaniae,* VII, 1004.

24 *Concilia Germaniae,* VII, 1072.

toms, life, and actions of his people, noting especially the frequency with which they received the sacraments. The spiritual and material needs of the poor, the orphans, the widows, and other similar classes of parishioners were to be looked into, as well as the friendship and morality among the women of the parish.[25] Here, then, was direct legislation on a parish census, though it was not taken necessarily in the door-to-door fashion as is now done. It must also be remembered that any legislation then passed as touching on a parochial spiritual status register implied that a census be taken, which after all was the only adequate means for the gathering of the required information.

Four years later, in Avignon, a Provincial Council made the same ruling that had been enacted at Tolouse, but in addition required the recording of the results in a book. So important was this considered that without it the pastor, and even the bishop, were not thought capable of performing their parocial duties.[26]

The legislation on the parochial spiritual status register and census became direct and specific in the Provincial Council of Salerno (1599), so much so as to urge the pastor to visit his flock each week in order to ascertain its needs.[27] At Narbonne (1609) it was suggested that the pastor frequently visit the infirm, and that he also inquire about those who were openly remiss in their faith or publicly regarded as usurers, adulterers, blasphemers, or excommunicates,[28] though no mention of the keeping of a book or record regarding this was made. The Provincial Council of Worms in 1610 supplied for this deficiency.[29]

Meanwhile, in 1604, the Congregation of Bishops and Regulars was called upon to solve the problem of whose right it was to care for the parochial books. The decision as given pointed out that it

[25] Hardouin, X, 1791.

[26] Mansi, XXXIV, 1354.

[27] Mansi, XXXV, 1008b.

[28] Mansi, XXXIV, 1513b.

[29] Concilia Germaniae, IX, 135.

was not only the right but the duty of the pastor, a right and duty which he could assert even against the bishop.[30]

To summarize this period in history it may be said that as a result of the interest shown by the Council of Trent a great deal of particular legislation began to appear in regard to the census and register. Especially detailed and finely drawn was that of the many Councils of Milan held under the guidance of St. Charles Borromeo. Therein almost every factor—who, when, where, what, by whom, and how—received proper attention. In the meantime, legislators of other lands were acting in a similar, though not as complete, a manner.

[30] S. C. Ep. et Reg., *Caven.,* 3 iun. 1604 — Pallottini, *Collectio omnium conclusionum et resolutionum quae in causis propositis apud Sacram Congregationem Cardinalium S. Concilii Tridentini interpretum prodierunt ab eius institutione anno MDLXIV ad annum MDCCCLX, distinctis titulis alphabetico ordine per materias digesta* (17 vols., Romae, 1868-1893), XII, p. 269, n. 66 (hereafter cited Pallottini).

CHAPTER V

THE *ROMAN RITUAL* AND ITS INFLUENCE

Article I: The Roman Ritual

With so much particular legislation existing on the question of parochial books, especially the parochial spiritual status register, it was not surprising to see the advent of a universal law on the subject. Since this is the first time the universal Church spoke on the subject, and inasmuch as its influence is felt to the present day, a detailed treatment seems in order. The memorable year that marked the climax in the development of legislation pertaining to the parochial spiritual status register was 1614. It was in that particular year that Pope Paul V (1605-1621) introduced to the Catholic world the *Roman Ritual.* Accompanying its publication with the Constitution *Apostolicae Sedi,* he wrote:

> Called by divine munificence, and not through any personal merit, to occupy the See of the Apostles, we deem it our duty to watch with full earnestness over all that concerns the decorum of God's house. And such increasing vigilance on our part prompts us to take suitable measures so that, as the Apostle admonishes, everything in divine worship may function decently and orderly . . . Pope Pius V, our saintly predecessor, fully conscious of his obligation which is now ours, labored with pastoral indefatigability to publish first the *Roman Breviary,* then the *Roman Missal* . . . so that there might be, God willing, a uniform manner of chanting and praying. . .
>
> With all this accomplished, there remained to be published, by authority of the Holy See, a volume of the *Ritual,* which would contain the genuine and sacred rites of the Catholic Church, those which must be observed by the shepherds of souls in the administration of the sacraments and in other ecclesiastical functions. Among the numerous existing rituals, it shall rank as the official and authorized one, by whose standard the officiants shall ful-

> fill their priestly office unhesitatingly, and with uniformity and precision . . . In order that the task might proceed in a correct and orderly manner ,as it should, we have assigned it to certain of our venerable brethern among the cardinals . . . Aided by the counsel of scholars and through comparison with ancient as well as other available rituals . . . the commission of cardinals has succeeded, after mature deliberation and with the help of God, in compiling a ritual of the desired brevity.
>
> Wherefore, we exhort in the Lord the venerable brother patriarchs, archbishops, bishops, and their vicars, beloved sons of ours, as well as abbots, all pastors wherever they labor, and all others concerned, as sons of the Roman Church, that in the future they use during the sacred functions this *Ritual,* selected as official by the authority of the same Church, mother and teacher of all; and that in a matter so important as this they observe inviolately whatever the Catholic Church and its ancient and approved usage and tradition have established.[1]

Thus, in one stroke, was introduced the uniformity so long needed. All, no matter who they were, or where they resided, were to observe fully the prescriptions of this *Ritual.* Here at last was to be found a general norm of action.

The great solicitude of the Council of Trent for the proper care of souls certainly found an admirable complement in the *Roman Ritual* of Paul V. In the very first title of the *Ritual, "De iis quae in sacramentorum administratione generaliter servanda sunt,"* it was stated that anyone held to administer the Sacraments ought to possess the necessary books pertaining to his office, "particularly those that were to be used for future reference as permanent registers

[1] *Codicis Iuris Canonici Fontes,* cura Émi Petri Card. Gasparri editi (9 vols., Romae; Typis Polyglottis Vaticanis, 1923-1939; Vols. VII, VIII, IX, ed. cura et studio Émi Iustiniani Serédi), n. 198 (hereafter cited ***Fontes***).

of the various parochial functions."[2] That this applied to the parochial books treated in the final title of the *Ritual* is explicitly noted. There, under the title *"De libris habendis apud parochos,"* five books are enumerated: the baptism, confirmation, marriage, and death registers as well as the parochial spiritual status register. Exactly the same words are used as are now found in canon 470,§1 in declaring that all five books are to be kept, and diligently used, according to the prescriptions of the Church or the proper ordinary.[3]

From the *Ritual* onward legislation no longer considered the registers merely *in globo*. Thenceforth the various books had a more definitely separate entity, thus allowing one, from that time to the enactment of the Code of Canon Law, to make each book the basis for a distinct study. Our concern, of course, is with the parochial spiritual status register.

The form described for this register in the *Roman Ritual,* since it remains in force to the present, is of such importance that, despite the risk of appearing repetitious, the writer offers the exact words:

> Familia quaeque distincte in libro notetur, intervallo relicto ab unaquaque ad alteram subsequentem, in quo singillatim scribantur nomen, cognomen, aetas singulorum, qui ex familia sunt, vel tamquan advenae in ea vivant. Qui vero ad sacram Communionem admissi sunt, hoc signum in margine e contra habeant: C. Qui sacramento Confirmationis sunt muniti, hoc signum habeant: Chr. Siqui ad alium locum habitandum accesserint, eorum nomina subducta linea notentur.[4]

A paradigm was then offered:

> Year. . . ., day. . . ., month. . . ., street. . . ., in the home of. . . . these dwell:

[2] *Rituale Romanum Pauli V Pont. Max. Iussu Editum,* cum Coniurationibus, et Benedictionibus variis, nunc addita Formula Absolvendi, et Benedicendi Populos et Agros, a Sacrorum Congregatione approbata (Romae: Typis et sumptibus Philippi de Rubeis, 1652), p. 2 (hereafter cited *Rit. Rom. Pauli V*).

[3] *Rit. Rom. Pauli V,* p. 321.

[4] *Rit. Rom. Pauli V,* pp. 324, 325.

C. *Chr.* Paul. . . ., Son of Peter, age. . . .
C. *Chr.* Appolonia, his wife, daughter of James. . . ., age. . . .
C. Dominicus, their son, age. . . .
C. Lucy, their daughter, age. . . .
C. Chr. Anthony, son of . . . ., a servant, age. . . .
C. Chr. Catherine. . . ., daughter of. . . ., a servant, age. . . .
Martin, son of. . . ., age. . . .

A definite change is to be noted. The *Ritual* makes no reference in the parochial spiritual status register to baptism or marriage (these presumbly received mention in other parish books), nor to annual confession. Up to the time of the *Ritual* the latter had been one of the main considerations of the parochial spiritual status register. The following will suffice to explain in some wise this change.

A long struggle had ensued between the secular and the religious clergy in view of the privileges which the latter had gained in regard to the right to hear the annual confession of the members of a parish. Pastors did everything in their power to maintain this exclusive right, but at length they had to yield. When the practice which abstracted from the pastor's exclusive right became generally accepted, the era of the registration of those who had made their sacramental confession came to an end.[5] Nevertheless the pastor was able to maintain his exclusive right over the administration of Paschal Communion till as late as 1905.[6]

Article II: Particular Legislation On The Census and the Spiritual Status Register

No outstanding modifications or additions to the prescriptions of the *Roman Ritual* are to be found in the subsequent legislation. Counciliar legislation and recourse to the various Sacred Congregations regarded the *Ritual* as the supporting principle. Frequently, enactments on such matters were introduced with the phase "*secundum*

5 Villien, *History of the Commandments of the Church* (St. Louis, 1951) pp. 176. 222.

6 The older observance ceased to continue as a law after the issuance of the decree *Sacra Tridentina Synodus* on Dec. 20, 1905, as stated in a reply of the S. C. C. Nov. 28, 1912. — *AAS,* IV (1912), 726.

Ritual Romanum," with their dependence on this general regulation duly noted. This is seen, for example, in Provincial Council of Benevento held in 1793, which insisted in addition that a copy be made and sent to the episcopal curia each year. Failure to comply with this order resulted in the infliction of a penalty to be determined by the respective bishop.[7]

No explicit mention of a register was found in the National Council of Albania (1703), but the pastor's obligation to know his parishioners was emphasized, with a listing of the things he was to look for. This list included all the information that was normally to be sought in the parochial spiritual status register.[8] The Provincial Council of Avignon (1725) went into much greater detail in restating the directives of the *Roman Ritual.* The pastor, to acquire information, was to visit his entire parish twice a year, and then follow up his finding with admonitions, corrections, and spiritual and material help wherever needed. Those who remained obstinate in their faults or sins were to be reported to the bishop, who would impose the proper penalties. Pastors failing to comply with this directive were subject to canonical correction.[9]

General legislation is found in the Constitution *Firmandis* of Benedict XIV (Nov. 6, 1744). This constitution imposed upon all bishops the obligation to check on the accuracy of the *"liber status animarum"* while on their regular visitation.[10]

The place set aside for the parochial books was of great interest to the Provincial Council of Cologne in the following year (1745). Each parish church was to have an archive or at least a place set aside in the sacristy for all such records, especially the spiritual status register. They were to be kept under lock and key, lest such important documents fall into the hands of undesirables.[11]

[7] *Acta et Decreta Sacrorum Conciliorum Recentiorum, Collectio Lacensis,* Auctoribus Presbyteris, S. J. e Domo S.V.M. sine Labe Concepta ad Lacum (7 vols., Friburgi Brisgoviae; Sumptibus Herder, 1870-1892), I, 72 (hereafter cited *Coll. Lacensis*).

[8] *Coll. Lacensis,* I, 324 b.

[9] *Coll. Lacensis,* I, 489 b.

[10] *Fontes,* n. 349.

[11] *Concilia Germaniae,* X, 549.

One question that remained to be settled became the subject of much controversy. That was the question of who had the right to keep the parochial spiritual status register. It has already been seen that even ten years before the introduction of the *Roman Ritual*, the Congregation of Bishops and Regulars had determined the care of the spiritual status register to be the exclusive right of the pastor. Nevertheless, since this was only a particular decision, the controversy continued in other dioceses throughout the world. For example, in 1762 the Bishops of Andria and of Ripatransone deemed it necessary to have recourse to the Sacred Congregation of the Council for a definite answer. Both replies of the Congregation reiterated the former direction that the pastor alone had the right to keep the parish registers, including the *"liber status animarum,"*[12]

Five years later, the filial church of St. Nicholas was instructed by the Sacred Congregation for the Propagation of the Faith to send yearly the parochial spiritual status register to the cathedral archives.[13] That such a ruling did not intend to infringe upon the pastor's exclusive right, but served rather as a safeguard measure for the books themselves, is evident from later decisions given by the Sacred Congregation of the Council to Ivrea in 1832 and to Montepulciano in 1856,[14] as well as from one given by the Congregation for the Propagation of the Faith in 1869, wherein, incidentally, the *Roman Ritual* was explictly referred to.[15] These decisions stated that the books were confided to the pastor's charge, and were, therefore, to be kept and guarded by him. Pallottini observed that if by statute copies of the parochial spiritual status register were to be sent to the curia, this was done with the thought of preserving a copy, should the regular parish records be lost or destroyed. [16]

In the meantime certain of the Councils of Baltimore (1829-1869) insisted that the register be kept according to the directives

[12] *Thesaurus Resolutionum, Sacrae Congregationis Concilii* (167 vols., Urbini, 1718-1741, Romae, 1741-1908), XXXI, 186 and 238 (hereafter cited *Thesaurus*).

[13] *Thesaurus,* XXXIX, 230.

[14] Pallottini, XII, 269.

[15] *Fontes,* n. 4876.

[16] Pallottini, XII, 268.

of the *Roman Ritual.* In the very first Provincial Council (1829) this regulation is found,[17] and is again repeated in the third (1837),[18] and fifth (1843).[19] The latter Council, moreover, gave its approval to the *Ritual* in the form in which it had been edited at the behest of the previous councils, and enjoined upon all pastors of souls the obligation to visit the infirm and the dying. The I Plenary Council for the United States, which was convoked in Baltimore in 1852, extended the enactments of the earlier Baltimore provincial councils to the entire United States, once again, explicitly mentioning the *Roman Ritual.*[20]

The I Provincial Council of Westminister (1852)[21] and those of Bordeaux in 1853[22] and 1859[23] not only insisted that the parochial status register be kept according to the *Roman Ritual,* but also indicated that the necessary information was to be gained by means of a pastoral visitation of the parish, hence through a parish census. In that way would the pastor have before his sight the progress made by the souls under his care.

The Provincial Councils of the Colonies of England, Holland, and Denmark in the West Indies, as held at Port of Spain in 1854[24] and 1867,[25] likewise required the register, a copy of which was to be sent annually to the bishop. So also did the Provincial Council of Ravenna (1855) require a *liber "secundum Rituale Romanum."*[26]

Though the II Provincial Council of Quebec in 1854 did not explicity legislate on the keeping of a register, it did require the pastor to know and visit his parishioners.[27] There was, however, explicit legislation at the Council of Vienna (1858)[28] and at

17 *Coll. Lacensis,* III, 28.
18 *Coll. Lacensis,* III, 57.
19 *Coll. Lacensis,* III, 90.
20 *Coll. Lacensis,* III, 145.
21 *Coll. Lacensis,* III, 941 b.
22 *Coll. Lacensis,* IV, 653 d.
23 Coll. Lacensis, IV, 760 a.
24 *Coll. Lacensis,* III, 1100 a.
25 *Coll. Lacensis,* III, 1114 c.
26 *Coll. Lacensis,* VI, 193 d.
27 *Coll. Lacensis,* III, 656 c.
28 *Coll. Lacensis,* V, 309 d.

the Council of Urbino (1859),[29] for these two Provincial Councils did demand parochial spiritual status registers *"secundum Rituale Roman"* as well as parish visitations. The latter Council is especially worthy of note inasmuch as it demanded "follow-up" work on the part of the pastor. Certainly the findings made by the pastor regarding the spiritual health of his flock could serve for suggesting the needed remedies for the correction of abuses and the reclamation of those who had lapsed from their faith.

The Provincial Council of Utrecht (1865) dealt mainly with the obligations of newly appointed pastors and first pastors of new parishes. These were to become acquainted, as soon as possible, with the parishioners through a census, the results of which were to be kept in the parochial spiritual status register. Again great emphasis was laid upon the necessity for pastors to know their flock intimately, so much so that a further ruling was made that this census be taken each year.[30] In New Granada, in 1868, provision was made by the Provincial Council for the pastor who, for one reason or another, was impeded from taking the yearly census. Rather than postpone it for a year he was to appoint someone else to do this work, recording the information thus obtained in the spiritual status register according to the directives of the *Roman Ritual*.[31]

An instruction, already referred to, of the Sacred Congregation for the Propagation of the Faith in 1869 charged vicars apostolic with the obligation of diligently and properly keeping the record of the condition of souls, especially with reference to the fulfillment of the Paschal precept.[32]

Finally, in 1875, the National Synod of Maynooth[33] and in 1883, the IV Provincial Council of New York[34] legislated, as had other Provincial Councils some years previous, that a parochial register be kept, as the *Roman Ritual* had directed. With this, the his-

[29] *Coll. Lacensis* VI, 46 c.

[30] *Coll. Lacensis*, V, 790 a.

[31] *Coll. Lacensis*, VI, 480 d.

[32] *Fontes*, n. 4876.

[33] *Acta et Decreta Synodi Plenariae Episcoporum Hiberniae Habitae apud Maynutiam* (1875) (Dublini: Typis Browne et Nolan, 1877), p. 113.

[34] *Acta et Decreta Concilii Provincialis Neo-Eboracensis* IV (1883) *Neo Eboraci: Typis Societatis pro Libris Catholicis Evulgandis*, (1886), p. 70.

torical treatment of all legislation on the parish census and parochial spiritual status register comes to a close.

Article III: Summary

By way of summary it may be said that, though the Council of Trent passed no legislation on the subject, it nevertheless gave the impetus to the whole movement by emphasizing the importance of a pastor's intimate knowledge of his flock. Gradually the particular councils enacted more specific legislation on the parochial spiritual status register by urging the pastor to construct its entries with a degree of detailed completeness. There was at first only a suggestion of the fact that the book, being a pastoral record, both spiritual and material, of the condition of the flock, was to be used as a basis for the alleviation of existing needs. The original purpose which the book served, that of registering the fact of yearly confession and Easter Communion, gradually lost all appreciable meaning. Rather with an extended purpose the register was to serve the gaining of a knowledge of the entire life, both spiritual and material, of the families, not just the individuals, in their respective parishes.

The *Roman Ritual* then introduced much needed uniformity. Not only did its prescriptions apply to all who were charged with the care of souls, but it even furnished a paradigm on which all such records were to be modeled in the future. Particular councils thereafter strongly insisted on a yearly visitation of all the homes in a parish with a view to having the record renewed annually. That the pastor had the exclusive right and duty in this regard was determined unanimously by the various Congregations of the Holy See in responses given to individual dioceses and bishops, as has been noted. The 19th century saw particular councils throughout the world emphasize the necessity of house to house visitations, and especially the necessity of "follow-up" work on the part of the pastors. By admonition, correction, and material or spiritual help, when possible, were those who were charged with the *cura animarum* to put to use information gained through the census and recorded in the parochial spiritual status register.

CANONICAL COMMENTARY

CHAPTER VI

Matter to Be Included in the Parish Census and the Parochial Spiritual Status Register

Article I: The Information to be Sought - Reasons

a) The parochial spiritual status register

In the previous chapter it was seen that the *Roman Ritual* of Pope Paul V was to be the official and authorized guide to be used in the universal Church with regard to the parochial spiritual status register. Since that time (1614) nothing has been added or changed in any way by the common law.[1] As a matter of fact the footnote of canon 470,§1, refers the reader to title X, chapter 6, of the *Roman Ritual* in regard to the form of this spiritual status register. There it is that one finds what information is to be included in this register.

> Familia quaeque distincte in libro notetur, intervallo relicto ab unaquaque ad alteram subsequentem, in quo singillatim scribantur nomen, cognomen, aetas singulorum qui ex familia sunt, vel tamquam advenae in ea vivunt. Qui vero ad sacram Communionem admissi sunt, hoc signum in margine e contra habeant: C. Qui Sacramento Confirma tionis sunt muniti, hoc signum habeant: Chr. siqui ad alium locum habitandum accesserint, eorum nomina subducta linea notentur.

Thus it is seen that the spiritual status register must contain the name, surname, and age of each person living in the parish along with a notation whether first Holy Communion and the Sacrament of Confirmation have been received. It is the opinion of O'Rourke in his treatment of this question that the listing as found in the *Ritual* is all-inclusive

[1] O'Rourke, *Parish Registers*, p. 41.

> Nothing further has a place in this register, and private information particularly is to be kept out of this official parochial record. If certain circumstances exist which affect families or members of families of the parish which a future pastor should know, said information must be given him orally or through other channels when necessary, not through this book.[2]

The writer, however, wishes to disagree with this viewpoint. A study of the purpose of the parochial spiritual status register leads him to regard the directive of the *Roman Ritual* as being exemplary or illustrative rather than actually comprehensive or all-inclusive.[3] It has already been noted elsewhere that the parochial spiritual status register is to be an up-to-date, accurate account of the condition of the souls in a parish.[4] It is to be an aid by means of which the pastor can, at a glance, ascertain the external progress of the souls in his care in their quest for perfection. Such occurrences as invalid marriages, failure to confess yearly, omission of the Easter Communion, lack of attendance at Sunday Mass, and general failure to practice one's religion have a direct bearing on this process. Specific instances of these abuses must be brought to and kept in the mind of the pastor. Otherwise it would be quite impossible for him to correct and give proper guidance.[5] Thus it is evident that if the very purpose of the parochial spiritual status register is to be gained,

[2] O'Rourke, *Parish Registers*, p. 83.

[3] *Cf.* Giraldi, *Animadversiones et Additamenta ex Posterioribus Summorum Pontificum Constitutionibus et Sacrarum Congregationum Decretis Desumpta ad Augustinum Barbosa, De Officio et Potestate Parochi* (*Romae*, 1774), Pars I, Cap. VII, n. 1, p. 61, (hereafter cited Giraldi); also Pirhing, *Jus Canonicum in V Libris Decretalium* (4 vols., Dilignae, 1722), Lib. I, tit. 31, n. 154 (hereafter cited Pirhing); Frassinetti-Hutch, *The New Parish Priest's Practical Manual* (2. ed., London and New York: Burns and Oates, 1885), p. 249 (hereafter cited Frassinitti-Hutch); Letter of Apostolic Delegate — June 12, 1941 — *Digest*, II, 149.

[4] *Supra*, p. 8; *also Barbosa, Pastoralis Sollicitudinis sive de Officio et Potestate Parochi Descriptio* (Lugduni: Sumptibus Philippi Borde, Laurentii Arnaud, et Claudius Regaud, 1655), Pars. I, Cap. VIII, p. 23 (hereafter cited *Pastoralis Solicitudo*).

[5] Cappello, *Summa Iuris Canonici* (3 vols., Vol. I, 5 ed., Romae: Typis Pontificiae Universitatis Gregorianae, 1951), I, n. 536.

then indeed considerations other than those specifically mentioned in the *Ritual* must be included.

A further indication of this viewpoint may be drawn from the Code and Canon Law itself. Canon 470,§1, provides that the spiritual status register be inscribed either according to the approved custom of the Church[6] or according to the particular prescriptions of the proper ordinary. Such liberty granted to proper ordinaries clearly implies that the addition of further information, not included in the *Roman Ritual*, is possible. Whenever he sees fit, the proper ordinary may add questions according to the needs of his diocese.

Since the points of information to be found in the parochial spiritual status register are for the most part identical with those which are to be sought in the parish census, these points will be treated under the latter heading and thus there can be avoided all unnecessary duplication,

b) The parish census

A complete parish census and parochial spiritual status register ought to include the following questions and answers:

1) Name—This should include the name and surname of every person living in the same household.[7] If two families with different names reside together, whether as relatives, or as employers and employees, this should be noted as is indicated in the *Roman Ritual*.

2) Address—If the family lives in an apartment house, the number of the apartment should be noted. The reason for including a notation of the address is self-evident. The pastor must know where he is to contact those with whom he must work.[8]

[6]Coronata, *Institutiones Iuris Canonici ad usum Cleri et Scholarum* (Altera editio, 5 vols., Taurini-Romae: Domus Editorialis Marietti, 1939-1947) I, n. 486 (hereafter cited Coronata); Baruffaldus, *Ad Rituale Romanum Commentaria* (2 vols., Florentiae: Sumptibus Editorum, 1847), II, nn. 96, 12: "Formulam describendi statum animarum in libro variari potest secundum consuetudinem locorum."

[7] *Rit. Rom. Pauli V*, pp. 324, 325.

[8] Mothon, *Institutions Canoniques* (3 *vols. Parisiis*, 1922-1924, *I, n.* 973 (hereafter cited Mothon).

3) Relationship to the head of the household—Here would be found a simple notation as, for example, wife, daughter, brother, sister-in-law, employee, etc.[9] Knowledge of an individual's relationship is practical for the pastor. Should he be called in to settle family disturbances, or should he need testimony concerning one of the members of a household under his care, etc., this knowledge of family ties would be of immeasurable aid.

4) Personal description—The proper recording of the ages of the individuals is also of great importance.[10] Such information is of value especially in regard to the reception of first Communion,[11] of Confirmation,[12] and of Matrimony.[13] Furthermore, individual studies[14] have shown that pastors must give additional attention to single people from the age of 20 to 29, and married people over 30 years of age, in regard to the fulfillment of their Easter duty. These groups are particularly lax in this obligation. If the parish contains mixed racial groups, the color or race should also be noted upon ascertainment thereof.[15]

Likewise it is of help to note the nationality of the persons living in the parish. While this may seem of relatively little importance, it does serve in part to explain the religious condition of certain Catholics.[16]

[9] C. Nuesse — T. Harte, *The Sociology of the Parish*, p. 246.

[10] *Rit. Rom. Pauli V*, pp. 324, 325.

[11] Canon 854 — Parocho est officium advigilandi. . .ne pueri ad sacram Synaxim accedant ante adeptum usum rationis . . .

[12] Canon 788 . . . ad septimum circiter aetatis annum . . . etiam antea si . . .

[13] Canon 1067. — Vir ante decimum sextum aetatis annum completum, mulier ante decimum quartum item completum, matrimonium validum inire non possunt.

[14] Kelly, *Catholics and the Practice of Faith* (Washington, D. C.: The Catholic University of America Press, 1946), pp. 89 and 58.

[15] Cf. J. G. McGroarty, "Census Findings in a Negro Parish," *The Catholic World*, CLVI (1942), 325-339.

[16] Schnepp, "Nationality and Leakage," *The American Catholic Sociological Review*, III (1942), 157-158; cf. also Ciesluk, *National Parishes in the United States*, The Catholic University of America Canon Law Studies, n. 180 (Washington, D. C.: The Catholic University of America Press, 1944); Shaughnessy, *Has the Immigrant Kept the Faith?* (New York: MacMillan Co., 1925).

Of course, the sex of the person should be noted in some way.[17] Very often it is impossible at a later date to determine this from the name alone, but it could well be learned from the recorded information regarding "relationship to the head of the household."

5) Education—There is every reason to believe that the practice of one's religion is positively related to educational attainment.[18] Hence it should be noted whether the individual received a grammer, high school, or a college education, and more important still, whether these schools were Catholic schools.[19] Naturally enough those possessing a Catholic education may be expected to be more faithful in their religious observance, and in fact to be the leaders among the Catholic laity. Hence the ones still of school age but not attending a Catholic institution should be reminded of their obligation in this regard.[20] Should it for some valid reason be impossible for a Catholic child to attend a Catholic school, mention should be made of the place and time where religious instructions are received.[21]

6) Economic Status—Every pastor should be concerned about the economic condition of his people, to alleviate their lot whenever it is within his power. Pope XI in his encyclical *Quadragesimo anno* uttered a judgement which is of interest to those who have the care of souls:

> These (temporal) goods ought indeed to be enough both to meet the demands of necessity and decent comforts and to

[17] *Supra,* p. 29.

[18] Pius XI, *Christian Education of Youth* . . . "education makes upon the soul the first, the most powerful and lasting impression for life, according to the well know saying of the Wise Man, "A young man according to his way, even when he is old, he will not depart from it. (Prov. 22:6)" *AAS* XXII (1930), 52.

[19] Navagh, *The Apostolic Parish* (New York: P. J. Kennedy & Sons, 1950), p. 108.

[20] Canon 1374. — Pueri catholici scholas acatholicas, neutras, mixtas, quae nempe etiam acatholicis patent, ne frequentent. Solius Ordinarii loci est decernere, . . . quibus adhibitis cautelis . . . tolerari possit ut eae scholae celebrentur; . . . also S. C. Prop. Fid., 6 Aug., 1867: ". . . in general no sufficient reason can be conceived for entrusting Catholic young people to non-Catholic universities." — *Fontes* n. 4868 (Vol. VII, p. 405). Cf. also response of Holy Office, 24 Nov., 1875 — *Fontes,* n. 1046 (Vol. IV, p. 362).

[21] Canon 1329. — Proprium ac gravissimum officum, pastorum praesertim animarum, est catecheticam populi christiani institutionem curare.

> advance people to that higher, happier and fuller condition of life, which when it is wisely cared for, is not only no hinderance to virtue, *but helps it greatly.*[22]

Every pastor is in a position to alleviate the distress of the poor. To do so, however, namely to provide charity, to help the unemployed find jobs, to distribute clothing and food to the destitute, to assist poverty-striken expectant mothers, etc., the pastor must know the facts.[23] The spiritual status register should provide those facts. For this reason it seems indicated to discern the occuption of the working members of the family,[24] as well as their approximate family income.[25] Care, however, must be shown in ascertaining the famly income. In most cases a direct question on this subject should be avoided lest resentment or suspicion be stirred up. It is possible very often to approximate the family income from the type of house, its furnishings, location, etc. Where questioning would seem out of place this is the better practice.

A less ascetic reason for inquiring into these matters, yet one of practical importance, has to do with the obligation of the parishioners to give financial support to the church.[26] The pastor who knows the approximate income of the families in his parish is able to plan church building and repairs for the future with an expected income budget.[27]

7) Religious Affiliation—Under this heading should be recorded the religion of the non-Catholics living in the parish.[28] Especially is this done in the case of mixed marriages. Though the priest may

[22] *AAS,* XXIII (1931), 202; English translation from *Two Basic Social Encyclicals* (New York: Benziger Brothers, 1943), p. 139.

[23] Navagh, *The Apostolic Parish,* p. 123; also Frassinetti-Hutch, p. 134; *Digest,* II, 148.

[24] Mothon, I, n. 973.

[25] Schnepp, "Economic Status and Leakage," *The American Catholic Sociological Review IV* (1943), 76-92.

[26] *A Catechism of Christian Doctrine, Revised Edition of the Baltimore Cathechism No.* 3 (Paterson, N. J.: St. Anthony Guild Press, 1949), p. 239.

[27] Navagh, *The Apostolic Parish,* p. 157.

[28] Canon 1350, §1, — Ordinarii locorum et parochi acatholicos in suis dioecesibus et paroeciis degentes, commendatos sibi in Domino habeant; Cf. also Coronata, II, n. 933.

fill in the space with the simple term "Non-Catholic," it is much more advisable to record the specific religion or religious preference of the non-Catholic, such as "Methodist," Episcopalian," "Baptist," etc. In the case of mixed marriages this information is important for the pastor, since he can use it to bring about a better understanding among the spouses and to afford the groundwork from which to begin a possible conversion.[29] If conversion of the non-Catholic party is impossible, at least a knowledge of his beliefs is essential to the zealous Catholic pastor who, when he visits such a home, would then be able to conduct himself accordingly.

Here, too, should the pastor note if any of the Catholic members of the family are converts. The presence of a convert in a family is an important fact which can serve the pastor in evaluating the religious condition of a family. Oftentimes the convert will be an outstanding Catholic, yet it sometimes happens, either through insufficient instruction or lack of conviction (frequently arising in conversions for the sake of marriage to a Catholic party) that such people will need special guidance. The pastor should try to determine whether special care is necessary and if so, note that fact in the register. This is especially important for the religious attitude of the whole family may be affected by the convert member, and generally is when the convert happens to be one of the parents. If those who are not yet converts show an interest in embracing the faith, but for one reason or another have never applied for instruction, this condition of things especially is to be inscribed in the register. In later visitations, the reason for their failure to seek instruction may be overcome, and a definite date set for the first formal lesson in Christian doctrine.[30]

8) Observance of Religious Duties—Under this category, without a doubt, are contained the most important questions to be asked and answers to be recorded. The record to be made of these matters is of the essence of the parish census and parochial spiritual status register.

[29] Shaughnessy, "Catholic Statistics and the *Status Animarum* Record," *ER*, C (1939), 107-108.

[30] Navagh, *The Apostolic Parish*, p. 146.

In the first place it must be ascertained if the person in question was ever baptized.[31] If the individual has never been baptized, a simple "No" could be marked in the space allotted. However, instead of simply writing a "Yes" in the event that he be baptized, it would be much better to write in the place of baptism. Not only would this reduce the possibility of a false or evasive answer, but when the parties are about to receive confirmation, to contract marriage, or to seek a dissolution of their marriage on some canonical grounds, there would be less delay in obtaining the baptismal certificate which is always necessary. The address from which it could be obtained would be as available to the pastor as his parochial spiritual status register.

Included also under the heading "Observance of Religious Duties" should be the fact of the reception of first Communion and Confirmation.[32] Since knowledge of the place where these were received is ordinarily of little value, the only exception being for those confirmed in infancy, it is generally sufficient to merely note the fact of their reception.

Then there could follow four specific questions in regard to the Easter duty, Confession, Holy Communion and Sunday Mass.[33] In regard to the Easter duty, the one taking the census should seek so to shape the question as to prevent all evasions in so far as that is humanly possible. For example, the priest might ask: "Where did you make your Easter duty this year?" or "On what day did you fulfill your Easter duty?" rather than simply asking "Did you fulfill your Easter duty?" When placing this information in the parochial spiritual status register, however, he need only mark the fact that the Easter duty was observed. The questions on attendance at Sunday Mass and on the reception of Penance and Holy Communion should also be phrased in such a way that a precise and objectively accurate answer is obtainable. Do you attend Mass regularly?" for example, reveals an unsatisfactory mode of questioning because of the very vagueness of the question. The use of such

[31] *Rit. Rom. Pauli V*, pp. 324, 325.

[32] *Ibidem*, pp. 324, 325.

[33] Giraldi, Pars I, Cap. VII, n. 1, p. 61; also Pirhing Lib. I, tit. 31, n. 154.

words as "regularly" and "generally" in the parish census gives the respondent too much room for evasion. A good census schedule and parochial spiritual status register is one that avoids general and indefinite terms.[34]

A better way of questioning and recording in this matter is the ascertainment of the number of times Sunday Mass was missed, for instance in the four weeks previous to the time of inquiry. By asking the respondent for his religious observance in any one month, the priest can have reasonable security that subjective answers will be avoided. The suggested phraseology, of course, assumes that the performance within a given month indicates year-round habits. As phrased, the questions may do an injustice to some individual, that is, a regular church-goer who may have missed Mass on one of two Sundays prior to the census, and yet has been faithful the rest of the year. The correct procedure in this case is to note his failure once or twice, as the case may be, but to add the fact that the respondent was otherwise faithful to this obligation. The same considerations apply also to the question of the reception of Penance and Holy Communion. However care must be taken by the enumerator not to probe too deeply and thus to ask questions that properly belong in the confessional.

Finally under the category of "Observance of Religious Duties" the pastor should ascertain the church at which the respondent attends services.[35] This question is particularly important when territorial parishes are in close proximity to one another, or when national parishes exist within the confines of a territorial parish.

9) Descriptions of Status.[36]—Because of the great importance here involved, a separate heading is advisable. The person's status, that is, whether he be single, married, widowed, separated, or divorced, should constitute the basis for the first question. Then for those who have declared that they are married there could follow questions on the date and place of the marriage ceremony.

[34] Lundberg, *Social Research* (New York: Longmans, Green & Co., 1942), p. 168.

[35] Francis, "The Dying National Parish and Compulsory Membership Registration," *ER*, LXXXXV (1936), 381.

[36] Navagh, *The Apostolic Parish,* 39; also Kelly, *Catholics and the Practice of the Faith,* 199; also Frassinetti-Hutch, pp. 134 and 249.

From this information the priest enumerator could in many instances immediately become aware of the validity or the non-validity of the marriage. Furthermore, if it is determined unfortunately that the marriage be invalid, the reason should be noted. Such information in the parochial spiritual status register would enable the pastor and the priests of the parish to learn if the marriage case is of a type that can be validated and to facilitate the handling of all cases of the same type without delay.

10) Catholic Societies—Though the roll book of every parish society will contain the names of its members, it is helpful to note the societies to which the individuals belong.[37] If they do not belong to a society, the pastor will see this at a glance, and be able to encourage them to join. If they are already members of one or more of the parochial societies, then he can encourage them to become more active in the work of the society. Such people, too, are more likely to co-operate with the pastor in other parochial undertakings. This in itself makes such a list useful.

The preceding questionnaire constitutes in general the basis for a complete parochial spiritual status register, and reflects the matter regarding which some information is to be sought in the taking of the census. Questions may be added to meet particular needs, but the questionnaire should never be made so long that it becomes unwieldy or tiring for the respondent nor should it include questions that belong properly to the confessional. However, it often happens that added information is more important than the data required by the schedule itself. The answers for these questions, should they be forthcoming, may be placed on the reverse side of the card. It must be kept in mind, however, that on only those points that are mentioned in the *Roman Ritual* does the general law of the Church require explicit questioning. The need of other information, as just presented in detail, springs from the purpose of the parochial spiritual status register and canon 467. Individual customs, diocesan status, and the regulations made by local Ordinaries must also be considered in this matter.

[37] Navagh, *The Apostolic Parish*, p. 115; for an opposite view cf. C. Nuesse — T. Harte, *The Sociology of the Parish*, p. 252.

Article II: Exemplary Forms

By way of comparison it may be of value to examine the resulting measure of difference between the census schedule (which constitutes a page of the parochial spiritual status register) now commonly in use and the complete one which has just been explained.

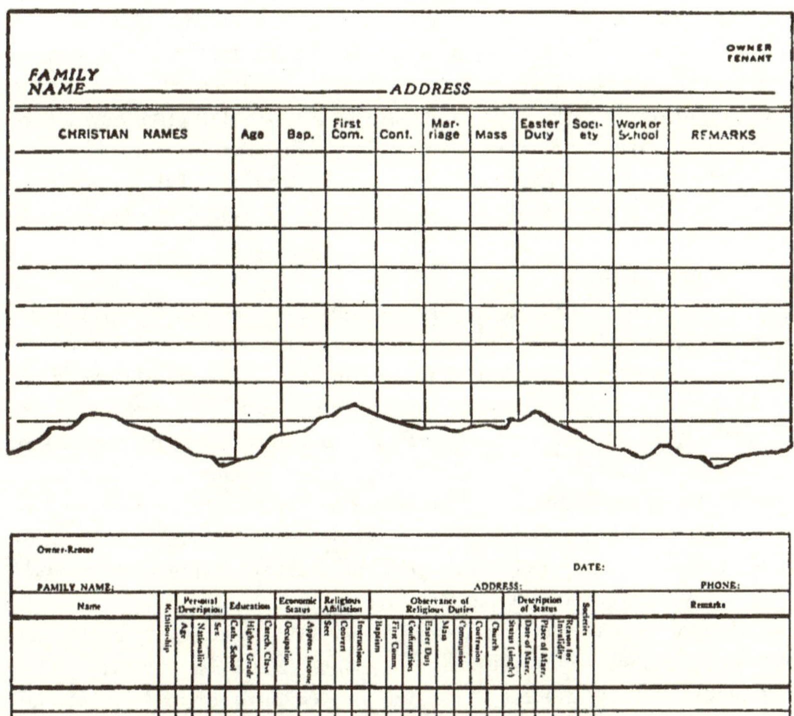

OWNER
TENANT

FAMILY NAME ______ *ADDRESS* ______

CHRISTIAN NAMES	Age	Bap.	First Com.	Conf.	Marriage	Mass	Easter Duty	Society	Work or School	REMARKS

Owner-Renter

DATE:

FAMILY NAME: ADDRESS: PHONE:

Name	Relationship	Personal Description			Education			Economic Status		Religious Affiliation			Observance of Religious Duties								Description of Status				Societies	Remarks
		Age	Nationality	Sex	Cath. School	Highest Grade	Catech. Class	Occupation	Approx. Income	Sect	Convert	Instructions	Baptism	First Comm.	Confirmation	Easter Duty	Mass	Communion	Confession	Church	Status (single)	Date of Marr.	Place of Marr.	Reason for Invalidity		

CHAPTER VII

PERSONS TO BE LISTED IN THE CENSUS AND THE SPIRITUAL STATUS REGISTER

Article I: Persons to be Included

Canon 470 does not explicitly treat the question of who are to be included in the parochial spiritual status register; it simply indicates the measure of the pastor's concern in the clause, *"pro viribus curet."* On the other hand, in regard to the parish census canon 467 makes the generic statement, *"debet parochus . . . suas oves cognoscere."* There is need here of a more definitive and clear-cut interpretation of these phrases. Fanfani in his comments on these clauses insists that each member of the faithful living in a parish is to be included in the census and the parochial spiritual status register.[1]

a) The parishioners

First, then, it is necessary to determine what is meant by a parish. The answer to this is twofold. Materially, the parish is the territory itself, circumscribed within definite limits, in which the resident faithful are under the care of a priest to whom the office has been given with the care of souls. Formally, the parish may be considered as the *coetus fidelium*, or the group of the faithful living in a definite territory under the care of a duly appointed priest.[2] Thus three essential elements are evident in the ordinary parish: a definite territory within a diocese, a group of the faithful living therein, and, finally, a proper pastor having the care of souls.[3]

These three elements are fully realized in a perfectly organized territorial parish or quasi-parish. Canon 216, §1, states: "The territory of every diocese is to be divided into district territorial parts; to each part is to be assigned its own church with a definite

[1] *De Iure Parochorum ad Norman Codicis Iuris Canonici* . (Taurini-Romae: Marietti, 1924), p. 71 (hereafter cited *De Iure Parochorum*).

[2] F. X. Wernz *Ius Decretalium*, II, 2.

[3] Bouscaren—Ellis, *Canon Law*, p. 151; Fanfani, *De Iure Parochorum*, p. 3; U. Beste, *Introductio in Codicem* (2, ed., Collegeville, Minn.: St. John's

part of the population, and its own rector who as the proper pastor of that territory is charged with the necessary care of souls." Paragraph three of the same canon points out that "the parts of a diocese mentioned in paragraph one are parishes. Should there be question of a vicariate or prefecture apostolic instead of a diocese, the parts of that vicariate or prefecture apostolic, if to them there has been assigned a specific rector, are quasi-parishes."

The Code, moreover, makes provision for parishes other than those purely territorial. "No change whatsoever is to be made unless the Holy See is consulted regarding parishes established for people of various tongues or nationalites dwelling in the same city or territory, and parishes created for certain families or persons. These parishes, however, no longer can be established without a special apostolic indult."[4] Thus, while frowning upon the future establishment of such parishes, the Church nevertheless recognizes the existance of a personal parish, i.e., one without distinct territorial limits, the population being determined by personal qualities alone, e,g., the people of a certain clan or family, and also what for lack of a better word may be called a mixed parish.[5] This latter type of parish consists of elements partly territorial and partly personal, e.g., when a parish exists for all the Italians resident within a certain territory.

In each of these three types of parishes—territorial, personal, and mixed—the parish census is to be taken and the parochial status register kept of each member living therein.[6] The problem, then resolves itself into a consideration of just what is to be understood by the expression "each member living therein."

The personal parish offers little difficulty. When a personal parish is established and a priest appointed as pastor of such a parish, the exact persons or families subject to his care are defined by the proper ecclesiastical authority.[7] The families or persons for whom it was established, and they alone, are to be included in its

Abbey Press, 1944), p. 225.

[4] Canon 216, §4.

[5] Bouscaren — Ellis, *Canon Law*, p. 152; Beste, *Introductio in Codicem*, p. 227.

[6] Canons 467 and 470.

census and parochial spiritual status register.

While a formal census may not be always necessary in such a parish, either because of the scarcity of its members, or because there are other means of personal contact between the pastor and his parishioners, the pastor must, nevertheless, keep on hand a current parochial spirtual status register of those in his charge. Personal parishes, however, are more the exception than the rule in the United States.

More in evidence are the territorial and mixed parishes, and these offer an additional problem in regard to the census and the parochial spiritual status register.

As regards the territorial parish, certainly all Catholics who have a domicile or a quasi- domicile within its borders are, as members of that parish, subject to the taking of a census and to having their names inscribed in the parochial spiritual status register.[8] The same is true in mixed parishes, due allowance of course being made for the added qualifications deriving from the elements of language and nationality.[9]

Those Catholics who possess more than one parochial domicile or quasi-domicile[10] present a special problem. However, since they are subject to each pastor, they are subject to the census and the parochial spiritual register in each parish. The reason for such a ruling follows from the fact that the law in no way limits the obligation incumbent on each pastor to include in his census and parochial spiritual status register *all* Catholics who possess a domicile or a quasi-domicile in his parish.[11] Hence the fact that his parishioners may have a domicile or quasi-domicile elsewhere in no way frees the pastor from his duty to include them, and conversely, they

[7] Beste, *Introductio in Codicem,* p. 225.

[8] Fanfani, *De Iure Parochorum,* pp. 65-71.

[9] *Loc. cit.*

[10] There can be no doubt that such a situation is possible. Cf. Woywod-Smith, *A Practical Commentary,* I, 50; Coroata *Institutiones Iuris Canonici,* I, n. 127; Vermeersch-Cruesen, *Epitome,* I, n. 212; Bouscaren-Ellis, *Canon Law,* p. 81.

[11] Fanfani, *De Iure Parochorum,* p. 71.

are obliged to cooperate with him by giving response to the questions he may ask while conducting the census.

b) *Vagi*

The Code rule that *vagi,* i.e., those who have no domicile or quasi-domicile, are under the jurisdiction of the pastor of the place where they actually happen to be,[12] and that they are bound by both, the general and the particular laws there in force.[13] Hence, should the pastor upon taking the census find *vagi* within his parish, he must by law determine their spiritual status as he would determine the status of those who have a domicile or a quasi-domicile within his parish, and he must record their names and spiritual condition in his parochial spiritual status register with the notation that they are *vagi.* It may be argued by some that the value of including *vagi* in this register is open to question because of their transitory character. Nevertheless the law is clear and it is the opinion of the writer that it must be followed.

Article II: Persons Who Are Excluded

a) *Peregrini*

Excluded from the parish census and parochial spiritual status register are all *peregrini,* i.e., those who are actually outside the place of the domicile or quasi-domicile which they still retain.[14] While such people are bound by the general laws of the place in which they happen to be, they are not bound by the particular laws of that place with the exception of only those laws which safeguard public order or determine the formalities of actions, e.g., contracts.[15] However, the general law regarding the census and the register is incumbent on pastors, not on the faithful.[16] Since the pastor of the place where these transients happen to be is not their proper pastor,[17] and has no claim to them as members of his church, he

12 Canons 91 and 94, § 2.
13 Canon 14, § 2.
14 Canon 91.
15 Canon 14, § 1.
16 Canons 467 and 470.
17 Canon 94, §1; Fanfani, *De Iure Parochorum,* p. 70.

is not in any way obliged nor does he have a right to include them in his census and parochial spiritual status register. Of their spiritual condition note is to be made rather by the pastor of their domicile or of their quasi-domicile.

b) Religious

Also excluded from the parish census and the parochial spiritual status register are all religious not only clerical, be they members of Orders or of Congregations, but also lay, both men and women, when exempted from the care of the pastor by law, by privilege, or by the ordinary.[18] Certainly the Holy See can do for the universal Church whatever a bishop can do for his diocese. Ordinaries can for a just and grave cause exempt from the care of a pastor religious communities and pious houses existing within a parish whenever the law itself has not exempted them.[19] Hence, if it pleases the Supreme Pontiff to take a group of the faithful or a community of religious from the care of a bishop or a pastor and to make them responsible only to himself or to someone delegated by himself, he may legitimately do so. Indeed, there actually are groups of religious both of men and women, who enjoy the apostolic privilege of exemption in whole or in part, from the jurisdiction of local Ordinaries and pastors. However, if the exemption is not absolute, but rather in some way limited, then in those things in which they are not exempted they remain under the jurisdiction of the Ordinary or the pastor.[20]

By law all *regulars,* both men and women, inclusive of novices and with the exception only of those nuns who are not subject to a regular superior, are exempt not only from pastors, but even from the local ordinary, save for the few exceptions that are stated in the law.[21] Hence the pastor would have no obligation to include them in his census and parochial spiritual status register even though their

18 Fanfani, *De Iure Parochorum,* p. 188; Creusen, *Religious Men and Women in the Code* (5. ed., Milwaukee: The Bruce Publishing Co., 1940), pp. 233 ff; Schaefer, *De Religiosis ad Norman Codicis Iuris Canonici* (4, ed., Roma: Editrice Apostolato Cattolico, 1947), p. 758 (hereafter cited *De Religiosis*).

19 Canon 464, § 2.

20 Fanfani, *De Iure Parochorum,* p. 189.

21 Canon 615.

house be situated within the limits of his territory. Those nuns who are not under the jurisdiction of a regular superior depend on the bishop himself who acts as a representative of the Holy See,[22] and as such also are exempt from the pastor's care.[23]

Postulants in these Orders, however, do not enjoy the privilege of exemption by law.[24] Rather are they to be placed on the same legal basis as lay people who live habitually with the members of a religious Order. Since the laity who dwell in a religious house at least a day and a night, whether by reason of employment, or with a view to education, or in the enjoyment of hospitality, or for the recovering of health, etc., nevertheless remain subject to their proper pastor, save only as regards Viaticum and Extreme Unction,[25] the same holds true for postulants in religious institutes. Thus are the above mentioned laity and postulants to be included in their proper pastor's census and spiritual status register.

All members, then, of religious Orders, inclusive both of priests and of brothers, and all nuns (those who have solemn vows) are to be omitted from the parish census and parochial spiritual status register. Only postulants and the laity residing at such religious houses remain subject to their proper pastor, and thus are to be accounted for in his census and register.

By privilege a few religious *Congregations* enjoy exemption. This, however, abstracts from the general rule, for the Code makes it clear that "institutes with simple vows do not enjoy the privilege of exemption unless it has been specially granted to them."[26] The Congregation of the Most Holy Redeemer (Redemptorist Fathers), and the Congregation of the Passion (Passionist Fathers) are among those few who enjoy this privilege. Other clerical congregations are exempted by the Code from the pastor's care regarding Viaticum and

[22] Creusen, *Religious Men and Women in the Code,* p. 235.

[23] S. C. de Religiosis, decr. 23 iun. 1923 — *AAS,* XV (1923), 357; also Schaefer, *De Religiosis,* p. 186.

[24] Crusen, *Religious Men and Women in the Code,* p. 235,

[25] Canon 514, § 1.

[26] Canon 618, § 1.

Extreme Unction,[27] funerals,[28] and the publication of the names of the *ordinandi*.[29]

Though no express concession of a general exemption of a *clerical* congregation from the pastor receives mention in the Code, and though there is no explicit expression of the revocation of parochial power, Schaefer, among others,[30] nevertheless concluded that both practice and doctrine favor such an exemption. His argument for the implicit exemption of religious is drawn from the fact that such congregations have by law the right to a church or an oratory of their own, as well as their own priest superior, who is able to take care of all of their spiritual needs. Hence it is altogether possible to contend that all clerical religious congregations, even though they be not exempt, are to be excluded from any parish census and parochial spiritual status register. This is not true, however, for postulants and laity residing with these congregations for the same reasons as given above in regard to religious Orders.

What, then must be said of non-exempt *lay* congregations, be they brothers or sisters with simple vows? Unless there be assigned to them a chaplain to whom the ordinary has given full parochial rights in accordance with canon 464, they remain under the care of the local pastor. Canon 464 allows the ordinary for a just and grave reason to exempt from the authority of the pastor a religious community or a pious institution located wthin the territory of a parish whenever they are not exempted by the common law. If this be the case, they would of course be exclude from the pastor's census and his parochial spiritual status register.

If they are not exempted by the Ordinary, they continue subject to parochial jurisdiction. This is clear from canons 514, § 3 and 1230, §5. On the face of this reasoning, it seems that they should be numered in the parish census and the parochial spiritual status register. However, because of the nature of the information sought in the census and recorded in the parochial spiritual status register.[31]

[27] Canons 514, § 1; 462, n. 3; 938, §2.

[28] Canons 514, § 4; 1221; 462, n. 5.

[29] Canons 998, § 1; 462, n. 4.

[30] Schaefer, *De Religiosis*, p. 186; Larraona "De Potestate Paroeciali Relate ad Religiosos," *Commentarium pro Religiosis*, VIII (1927), 38.

[31] Cf. *supra*, p. 45 ff.

such an inclusion seems to the writer to be unnecessary and impractical for lay and non-exempt religious. Moreover, canon 595 places upon all religious superiors the obligation to see to it that members of their communities are faithful to their religious exercises: the yearly retreat, daily Mass and mental prayer, weekly confession, frequent Communion, etc. So while it is true that the local pastor has the spiritual care of the members of these lay religious congregations, the exercise of it must proceed in harmony with the control which the law grants to the religious superior. The Code places the primary obligation upon the religious superor, though the pastor has the concomitant duty of making the reception of the sacraments available for the religious. Accordingly it appears that such religious need not be included in the pastor's census and parochial spiritual status register.

c) Societies of the common life

Societies, whether of men or of women, whose members, whether clerical or lay, live in common without vows are also exempt from the pastor's census and register in the same way as are the previously mentioned religious. This is evident from canons 675 and 679, which refer to the previous canons dealing with the position of religious in regard to their pastors.

d) Those who live in seminaries

Seminaries, and all who live therein, the faculty, the students, the sisters and other employees, are likewise exempt from all local parochial jurisdiction and by the same token do not call for inclusion in the census and the spiritual status register of the pastor in whose territory the seminary is situated. With due exceptions that relate to marriage and confession,[32] the parochial office is to be performed by the rector of the seminary or his delegate.[33] The exemption in general applies to major and minor seminaries, even though other than clerical students also attend it, and also to the seminary villa, even though this be in another diocese.[34] However,

32 Canon 891.

33 Canon 1368.

34 Bouscaren-Ellis, *Canon Law,* p. 702.

if those who live in the seminary retain a domicile or a quasi-domicile elsewhere, the pastor of that domicile or quasi-domicile ought to include them in his census and register.

e) Persons in the armed services

If a military reservation having its own chaplain lies within the limits of a parish, then there is no need in general for the local pastor to include the subjects of the chaplain in the census and the parochial spiritual status register. Included among the subjects of such a chaplain are those who are in the armed forces, their wives, and other relatives who reside in the same house with them, and all civilians living within the limits of the military reservation.[35]

Though the local pastor's jurisdiction is cumulative with that of the chaplain within the premises occupied by the armed forces, the ecclesiastical jurisdiction is to be exercised primarily by the chaplain and only secondarily, though in his own proper right, by the local pastor. This right is derived from the fact that the military personnel acquire a domicile in the parish in which the military reservation is situated.[36] Likewise one finds among the "Rules to be Observed by Military Chaplain" that at the end of each month the chaplain must send to the Military Chancery and to his own proper Vicar Delegate a report concerning the spiritual status of his own subjects.[37] In view of these facts it seems clear that the military personnel and such as are included among the subjects of a chaplain need not be included in the local parochial census and register though they may be. Only when they acquire or have a domicile or a quasi-domicile off the military reservation does there arise any need for the pastor of that domicile or quasi-domicile to include them in his census and the parochial spiritual status register.

f) Non-Catholics

Finally, a consideration of the non-Catholics living in a parish is in order. Canon 1350 commends non-Catholics to the care of the local Ordinary and pastor in whose diocese and parish they are living. The question naturally arises: "To what extent must the pastor exer-

[35] "Military Faculties" — *Digest,* II, 587.

[36] *Digest,* II, 589; *AAS,* XLIII (1951), 562.

[37] "Rules to be observed by Military Chaplains" — *Digest,* II, 619.

cise his care in their regard?" Vermeersch-Creusen[38] in answer, emphasize the caution shown by the Code in its statement: *commendatos sibi in Domino habeant acatholicas."* Carefully and with clear intent was the word "conversion," omitted lest the charge of proselytizing be levied against the Church and thus there should result more harm than good. Beste,[39] too, in noting this point, condemns any and all indiscrete zeal. Rather, he says, should the pastor by prayer and good example, and by the diffusion of apologetical books and pamphlets, reduce any prejudice on the part of infidels and heretics, and lead them on the road to God. The judgement as to whether stronger means are needed remains within the discretion of the individual pastors. In any case the obligation resting upon pastors in regard to non-Catholics is a grave one in charity,[40] and must be fulfilled according to their prudent judgment.

To extend the regulation of canon 1350 so as to include non-Catholics in the parish census and the parochial spiritual status register seems to be more than the law requires.[41] However, since the pastor has the non-Catholics commended to his care, he should at least know of them. Hence while there is no strict obligation to include them in any census, to include them could prove of likely benefit. In taking his first census the pastor would have to visit all the homes in the parish anyway in order to determine if anyone living therein is or ever was a Catholic. The while he is on such visits it would be rather easy for him to ascertain the family name and the sect to which the members of the family belong. From his conversation with them he would further be able to determine in a more or less general way their attitude toward the Catholic Church. A separate register similar to the parochial spiritual status register in form, but containing different information—family name, name of the sect, attitude toward the Church, and any other pertinent remarks--could then be drawn up by the pastor. The usefulness of such a register is self evident.

It is also possible to conceive that once the pastor has visited all the homes in his parish, both Catholic and non-Catholic,

[38] *Epitome,* II, n. 683.

[39] *Introductio in Codicem,* p. 658.

[40] Coronata, *Institutiones Iures Canonici,* II, n. 933.

[41] Beste, *Introductio in Codicem,* pp. 658-659.

subsequent censuses could be confined to visiting only the residences of all Catholics and the residences of those non-Catholics who were well disposed to his previous visit. Certainly no pastor can be obliged to visit people of other faiths when he knows harm will result to the church in general. Should new homes be built in the meantime by families unknown to the pastor or should houses be rented by families new to the parish, it goes without saying that these families too must be included in the subsequent census.

Article III: Summary

In summary, it must be said that all who have a domicile or a quasi-domicile within a parish, and do not at the same time belong to a mixed or a personal parish therein, as well as all *vagi* who happen to be within a territorial parish are persons to be included in the parish census and the parochial spiritual status register of the territorial parish. Mixed parishes have their own members based on territory and nationality, and personal parishes uniquely have their own members regardless of territory. These members are to be included accordingly in the census and register of the national or personal parish. Excluded are *peregrini*, religious and all non Catholics, as well as those who live in seminaries and on military reservations under the conditions already explained.

CHAPTER VIII

THE OBLIGATION OF TAKING THE CENSUS AND OF KEEPING THE REGISTER

ARTICLE I: GRAVITY OF THE OBLIGATION

The pastor with the care of souls has many and grave obligations and duties toward the people entrusted to his care. His pastoral obligations to them bind in strict justice.[1] In the whole gamut of these parochial obligations the duties mentioned in canon 467 and in canon 470 are among the principal and most important.[2]

Included within these canons is mention of the pastoral obligations of knowing each parishioner and of keeping a parochial spiritual status register. There can be no doubt that a serious and prolonged negligence in either one of these obligations brings with it grave spiritual harm to the souls of the parishioners. The pastor as a spiritual shepherd is bound to "know his sheep" in order to be able to "feed them." He must know who they are, and he must recognize what are their spiritual needs. In their very nature these obligations are of a grave character.[3]

Since the supreme law of the Church is the salvation of souls, it is the mind of the Church that any of its ministers, who by negligence and carelessness make the realization of this aim difficult,

[1] Canons 464, § 1, and 682; Fanfani, *De Iure Parochorum,* p. 3; Coronata, *Institutiones Iuris Canonici,* I. n. 480.

[2] Wernz — Vidal, *Ius Canonicum,* II, 939; cf. also *Digest,* II, 148.

[3] Augustine, *Commentary,* VII, 465; Aertnys — Damen, *Theologia Moralis secundum doctrinam S. Alfonsi De Ligorio Doct. Ecclesiae* (16 ed. Romae: Marietti, 1950), I, 813; Vermeersch, *Theologiae Moralis* (4 vols., Vols III, 4 ed., Roma: Typ. Pontificiae Universitatis Gregorianae, 1948), III, 64. It has remained a disputed matter whether the parochial spiritual status register is more rigorously prescribed than the other four registers mentioned in canon 470. Blat (*Commentarium Textus Codicis Iuris Canonici,* II, 437) thought so, but Chelodi (*Ius de Personis iuxta Codicem Iuris Canonici* [Tridenti, 1922], p. 228) took an opposite stand.

[4] Suarez, *De Remotione Parochorum,* n. 193; Coronata, *Institutiones Iuris*

be checked before the harm becomes irreparable.[4] Hence the Code is quite explicit in its regulations regarding such negligence. If a pastor grossly neglects or violates the pastoral duties described in canon 467, the bishop is empowered, nay even obliged, to admonish him, reminding him of his strict obligation of conscience and the penalties which the law decrees against these offenses.[5] If after receiving the bishop's warning the pastor does not amend, he is liable to a further rebuke and an appropriate penalty in proportion to his guilt.[6] Should this too prove unavailing, he may be deprived of his parish, in accordance with the canonical prescriptions for the removal of pastors.[7]

Concerning canon 470, the Code states that a pastor, who does not keep or preserve the parochial records diligently as the law perscribes that he should, be punished by his proper ordinary in proportion to the gravity of his guilt.[8] Not only may the pastor fail in this regard through various omissions and through careless and perfunctory performances of positive acts, but also by doing or permitting to be done certain forbidden acts. Canon 2406 comprehends this in declaring that "any person who is bound by his office to draft, write, or preserve . . . parochial books, and who presumes to falsify, mutilate, destroy, or hide them, is to be deprived of his office or punished with other grave penalties by the ordinary in charge of such records or books, and those who maliciously refuse, when legitimately requested, to transcribe, transmit, of exhibit those books, or who in any other way abuse their office, are likewise to be punished." This punishment may include deprivation of or suspension from office,

Canonici, III, n. 1575.

[5] Canon 2182.

[6] Canon 2183.

[7] Canon 2184. — Si et correptio et punitio in irritum cesserint, Ordinarius, probata, ad normam can. 2183, perseverante ac culpabili officiorum paroecialium omissione vel violatione in re gravi, parochum amovibilem sua paroecia statim privare poest; parochum vero inamovibilem beneficii fructibus, pauperibus ab Ordinario distribuendis, pro gravitate culpae in totum vel ex parte privet. Canon 2185. — Mala voluntate persistente ac probata, ut supra, Ordinarius etiam parochum inamovibilem e sua paroecia removeat.

[8] Canon 2383.

and money fines levied at the discretion of the ordinary in proportion to the gravity of the guilt.

It is evident, then, that the Church looks upon the taking of a parish census and the keeping of a parochial spiritual status register as being one of the most serious obligations incumbent on every pastor. Before the bishop can rightly apply the canonical penalties for failure in this regard, however, it is necessary that the pastor's neglect or forbidden action be not only a morally culpable but also a grave violation.[9]

To determine the gravity of such negligence or violation of the law is often a difficult task. It is practically impossible to give a general rule that will encompass each of the various negligences and violations. There are, however, some general notions that will be of help in determining if the negligence of the pastor in some given case is grave. This gravity—the serious harm occasioned for souls—is determinable not only through a proper appraisal of the pastoral obligations, but also through a due consideration of the attendant circumstances with reference to the factors of time, place and person.[10]

However, it is not necessary that scandal or actual injury in every case result from the negligence or the violation.[11] Accordingly to estimate the measure of the gravity in the negligence or the violation, it is necessary to use the norms established by moral theologians, by approved authors, and in the pratice of the Holy See.[12] Practically considered, the only general rule that can be given is that in the final analysis the gravity is to be estimated according to the prudent judgement of the ordinary, who must take into consideration the norms just mentioned. In addition, he should make use of the ordinary sources of information in ascertaining the fact of negligence. Rural deans, parish visitors, and the curates who are associated with the negligent pastor may well be consulted in this

[9] Canons 2182 and 2218, § 2.

[10] Canon 2196; Fanfani, *De Iure Parochorum,* p. 345; Wernz — Vidal, *Ius Canonicum,* VI, n. 789; Augustine, *Commentary,* VII, 467; Vermeersch-Creusen, *Epitome,* III, n. 370.

[11] Canon 21.

[12] Coronata, *Institutiones Iuris Canonici,* III, n. 1622; Vermeersch-Creu-

matter. Complaints and denunciations are to be duly evaluated.[13] Diocesan laws, legitimate customs, the location and the type of the parish, all should be considered by the ordinary in estimating the fact and the gravity of negligence.[14]

In all these considerations it must be remembered that the negligence or the violation here considered is had only when there is an habitual omission or violation, for a single omission would not constitute grave neglect as such. Moreover, this negligence or violation must have the nature of a canonical delict, which means in effect that the pastor must be guilty of mortal sin. Consequently for an evaluation of the gravity, those causes which lessen the imputability and the juridic effects of the delict should be kept in mind, such as ignorance, error, physical inability, and the like.[15] With these general principles in mind, the ordinary can arrive at a judgement whether the negligent pastor is subject to the canonical penalties attached to such negligence.

Article II: Role of the Local Ordinary

Although the pastor, by virtue of his office, has the care of the souls entrusted to him, his power is not absolute and independent; rather, it is necessarily subordinate to the jurisdiction of his ordinary and, of course, of the Roman Pontiff.[16]

As has just been seen, the ordinary has the right and the duty to inflict canonical penalties on a pastor who has been delinquent in regard to the parish census and the parochial spiritual status register. Furthermore the ordinary has the obligation, which he may fulfill either personally or through a delegate, to inspect the register at the time of the canonical visitation or at some other suitable time.[17]

sen, *Epitome,* III, n. 370.

[13] Cf. canon 1645, §1, regarding anonymous complaints.

[14] Coranata, *Institutiones Iuris Canonici,* III, n. 1622; Augustine, *Commentary,* VII, 466; Wernz — Vidal, *Ius Canonicum,* VI, n. 789.

[15] Cf. Canons 2199 — 2210.

[16] Canons 451, §1, and 218. In law the term ordinary includes the Roman Pontiff, and for his own territory a residential bishop, an abbot or a prelate *nullius* along with the vicar general of these, an administrator, and also a vicar or a prefect apostolic.

[17] Canon 470, §4; Benedictus XIV, *Firmandis,* (Nov. 6, 1744) — *Fontes,* n. 349.

According to the Third Plenary Council of Baltimore (1884), this visitation must take place at least once in every three-year period.[18] It seems, then, that the proper interpretation of "some other suitable time" must make it fall within the restriction of a three-year period. In other words, though the ordinary need not inspect the register while he is actually on his canonical visitation, he should inspect it sometime during each three-year period.

But even more than the mere right to inspect the register and to punish the pastor for his failure to have a register or to have one that is complete and up-to-date, the ordinary has the right to prescribe the manner in which the register is to be inscribed and preserved[19] He it is who determines what other information is required besides that which is called for by the *Roman Ritual* of Paul V,[20] the time within which it is to be renewed, the form which is to be followed and, in general, how it is to be maintained.

In the same way, the ordinary has the right and the obligation to see that the pastor knows his people, and accordingly that the pastor takes a parish census. This too, should be a point of inquiry while the ordinary makes his canonical visitation.[21] If he finds the census incomplete or that it was not recently assembled, it is then left to him, by careful questioning and evaluation of the answers given, to determine if a canonical penalty can and must be inflicted, and in general what course of action is to be taken. This the ordinary may also do even though the pastor be a member of a religious community.[22] While the purpose of the visitation is primarily aimed not at the infliction of punishment but rather at the preservation of sound and orthodox doctrine, the maintenance of good morals, the promotion of peace and harmony, and in general the aiding of

[18] *Acta et Decreta Concilii Plenarii Baltimorensis III* (Baltimore: John Murphy, 1886), n. 14. Canon 343 requires the ordinary to make an official visitation of the diocese, partial or complete, yearly, completing the rounds at least every five years. Particular law takes precedence in this case.

[19] Canon 470, §1.

[20] Cf. *supra*, p. 46.

[21] Slafkosky, *The Canonical Episcopal Visitation of the Diocese,* The Catholic University of America Canon Law Studies, n. 142 (Washington, D. C.: The Catholic University of America Press, 1941) p. 128.

[22] Canon 631, §1 and§2.

religion in every way possible,[23] correction and punishment, when they prove necessary, ought to be employed.

The question now arises regarding the fulness of the extent to which the ordinary may go in regard to the parish census and the parochial spiritual status register. It has been noted elsewhere that he is to see that these matters are diligently cared for by the pastor to the extent of inflicting canonical punishment if necessary, that he determine beyond the requirements of the *Roman Ritual* the information to be sought on the census and recorded in the parochial spiritual status register, and that he regulate the manner in which this information is to be maintained and preserved. It will also be seen that it remains for him to determine the frequency with which the census is to be taken and the spiritual status register renewed.

But does the ordinary have the right to interfere with the plan and practice of a pastor who is diligently taking the census and keeping an up-to-date accurate parochial spiritual status register according to his directives? In other words, may the ordinary inform such a pastor that a religious community, e.g., the Missionary Helpers of the Sacred Heart, will henceforth take the census in the pastor's parish, and that one of the curates will henceforth have charge of the parochial spiritual status register? To answer this question it is necessary to distinguish between the parish census and the parochial spiritual status register.

The keeping of the latter is more than a mere obligation binding upon the pastor; it is his exclusive right. When a case very similar to the one just mentioned in regard to the register arose and was sent to the Congregation of Bishops and Regulars, this Congregation in 1604 replied that the care of the parochial books was the right and the duty of the pastor, a right and duty which he could assert even against the bishop.[24] Though this was a particular decision and was given before the advent of the *Roman Ritual* of Paul V, it clearly evidenced the mind of the Church. Other particular decisions given after the appearance of the *Roman Ritual* by the Sacred Congregation of the Council in 1762 to the Bishops of Andria and

[23] Canon 343, §1.

[24] Pallottini, XII, p. 269, n. 66.

of Ripatransone[25] were to the same effect. The same solution was implied in later decisions of the same Congregation directed to the diocese of Ivrea in 1832, and the diocese of Montepulciano in 1856, [26] and by a decision of the Sacred Congregation for the Propagation of the Faith in 1869.[27]

Since the law regarding the keeping of the parochial spiritual status register as found in canon 470, §1, is in harmony with the first edition of the *Roman Ritual* of Paul V which appeared in 1614, it seems that in virtue of canon 6 (canons which restate the pre-Code law are to be interpreted as they were understood in this earlier law) the care of the parochial register even today is an exclusive right of the pastor. It is to the pastor, and to him alone, that the Code entrusts the parochial spiritual status register. The keeping of it is a duty attached to the very office of the pastor. Hence the ordinary cannot take the care of the register from him. The bishop's work is rather to see that the pastor fulfills his obligation in a correct manner. Even if the pastor is in some way negligent, the bishop may not take this right from him without removing him as pastor.

It likewise seems beyond the power of the bishop to compel a pastor, when he is faithful and diligent in the work of the census, thenceforth to use a group, e.g., the Missionary Helpers of the Sacred Heart for assembling the census. Similiarly the bishop cannot rightly constrain the pastor to cease in this work. The reason is clear—the census implies the enjoyment of a cumulative right in which both the pastor and the ordinary have a share.[28] Only if the pastor fails in his duty would the ordinary have the right, nay even the obligation, to assign a substitute to do this all-important work which is so necessary for the proper care of souls. Yet it must be noted that there is nothing contrary to law in the idea of a bishop forming a diocesan program for his own information, as long as he likewise recognizes the pastor's right and duty to take a census of all those who are under his parochial care.

[25] *Thesaurus,* XXXI, 186 and 238.

[26] Pallottini, XII, 269.

[27] *Fontes,* n. 4876.

[28] Canons 451 and 355.

ARTICLE III: PERSONS ON WHOM THE OBLIGATION RESTS

a) By way of personal fulfillment.

There can be no question that the obligation to take the parish census and keep the parochial spiritual status register rests directly upon the pastor.[29] Through his appointment he is given a parish *in titulum* with the care of souls.[30]

However it is necessary to note that not only a validly ordained priest but an ecclesiastical moral personality can be vested with the title of pastor.[31] It is not of infrequent occurrence that parishes actually are held in title by ecclesiastical moral personalities, especially by religious communities. In such cases the moral personality cannot itself be the actual pastor.[32] Rather must it provide a vicar into whose hands the actual care of souls is placed. For example, when a clerical religious community is given a parish, not all the the priests pertaining to that community can be regarded as having the actual spiritual care of the people committed to them. Otherwise the way would be paved for confusion and inefficiency in the care of the people's spiritual welfare. It is for this reason that the Church insists the actual charge of the parish be given to a single member of the community, the *vivarius actualis*.[33]

Such vicars, when charged with the care of parishes entrusted to religious communities or to other moral personalities, possess by law all the rights and duties that attach to the pastoral office. These rights and duties are specified not only by the common law, but also by diocesan statues and legitimate usage.[34] Any ruling, therefore, that is made for pastors is binding also upon vicars in the same manner unless the contrary be expressly stated. Since nothing to the

29 Canons 470, §1, and 467.

30 Canon 451, §1.

31 Canon 451, §1; Bouscaren-Ellis, *Canon Law,* p. 189; Fanfani, *De Iure Parochorum,* p. 72; Koudelka, *Pastors, Their Rights and Duties,* The Catholic University of America Canon Law Studies, n. 11 (Washington, D. C.: The Catholic University of America, Press 1921), p. 11; Coronta, *Institutiones Iuris Canonici,* I, n. 467; Vermeersch-Creusen, *Epitome,* I, nn. 538, 539.

32 Canon 452.

33 Canon 471, §4.

34 Loc. cit.

contrary is found in the common law, vicars may be said to have an obligation to take the parish census and to keep diligently the parochial spiritual status register just as any individual pastor.

Should the *vicarius oeconomus* or parish administrator be numbered also among those who have the obligation to take the census and to keep the spiritual status register? Placed as he is in charge of a parish vacant through the death or removal of its pastor,[35] to him are given all the rights and duties that belong to a canonical pastor as far as the care of souls is concerned until the new pastor has been appointed.[36] Hence it would appear that he too has the obligation to take the census and to keep the register.

The latter part of the same canon ,however, qualifies this broad statement by prescribing that the administrator do nothing which would be to the prejudice of the rights of the incoming pastor of the parish itself. [37] It is not difficult to see the possibility of such prejudice arising in a house to house census. Moreover, the appointment of administrators is generally made for a short period of time. Should the administrator foresee that his appointment will extend only over a few months it appears to the writer that there is little point in his beginning a parish census. Why oblige him to begin something that he cannot complete? The personal contact of the administrator with the few parishioners he would be able to visit and any knowledge he may acquire therein would be of little value to the incoming pastor who must conduct his own census. The obvious conclusion is that such an administrator (appointed for a short period of time) though having the rights and duties of a pastor, is freed from the obligation of taking a census and of keeping a spiritual status register.

If, however, an ordinary deems it necessary to appoint a priest as administrator of a parish for year's duration or longer, and the administrator finds among other things that the census and spiritual status register have been negelected for many years, it would seem as if the administrator would then have an obligation to begin a census and keep a register in an effort to reclaim the neglected flock. This of course, follows from the fact that he has entrusted to him the

[35] Canon 472, § 1.

[36] Canon 473, §1.

[37] Canon 473, § 2.

care of souls and any neglect on his part will result in further spiritual harm to those souls. A *status quo* cannot be permitted when conditions are such as to require rectification.

What of the *vicarius adjutor* or parochial adjutant? As the name implies, the parochial adjutant is an ordained helper given by the ordinary to a pastor who has either become too old and feeble to care for the parish properly, or who is afflicted with some permanent malady which hinders him in the fulfillment of his parochial duties.[38] Need such a vicar conduct a census and retain a spiritual status register?

When the adjutant takes the place of the pastor in all things, then he has by law also all the rights and duties of the pastor, except that of applying the *Missa pro populo.* It follows then that he would be obliged in general to take the parish census and to care for the parochial spiritual status register. Since the adjutant's appointment is generally of a much longer duration than that of the administrator, sometimes extending over a period of many years, and since there is no question of prejudicing the rights of the pastor who is present, there is all the more reason to oblige him to conduct a census and to keep a register.

However when as often happens, the adjutant supplies the pastor only in some of his parochial duties, then he does not possess by law all the rights and duties of the parochial office. In this case it will have to be determined from the letter of appointment whether he must care for the census and the parochial spiritual status register.[39]

It may frequently happen that the pastor is called upon to leave the parish for a time, e.g., because of ill health, for a vacation, in consequence of temporary suspension from office, etc. According to canon 465, §§4-5, if such a departure extends for more than a week, then a capable substitute must be provided. This substitute is called the *vicarius substitutus,*[40] and for the care of souls he has all the rights and duties that belong to the pastor himself, unless the ordinary

[38] Canon 475, §1; Bastnagel, *The Appointment of Parochial Adjutants and Assistants,* pp. 115 ff.

[39] Canon 475, § 2.

[40] Canon 474.

or the pastor explicitly reserve some of them. Yet there can be no doubt that substitute vicars are generally exempted from the pastoral obligation of starting a census and keeping a spiritual status register.

The reasons are evident. First, the period of time within which the substitute vicar as such will remain in the parish is generally of so short a duration that he cannot possibly see the work of a census through its ultimate completion. Secondly, he would have little or no knowledge of the parish, geographically or spiritually, nor would he be aware of the homes already visited by the pastor, nor the method employed by the pastor in conducting the census and recording the information. The result would only be confusion. Finally, it cannot be shown that the knowledge acquired by the substitute vicar will be of so great a benefit to souls as to outweigh the possible resultant prejudice to the rights and good name of the pastor. The pastor may have other means of knowing his flock, not evident to the substitute vicar, and the fact that the substitute may begin to take a census can easily cause wonderment among the faithful as to why their own pastor has not done so. Only if it is foreseen that he will remain as substitute vicar for a notable time, e.g. a year or more, and no harm would result to the pastor, would there be any obligation for the vicar to institute a census. In any case, however, he does have the right and even the obilgation to see to it that the assistant (*vicarius cooperator*), if committed to him, and he himself, if directed by the pastor, continue a census which was begun by the absent pastor and said assistant.

Besides pastors and permanent vicars, it is incumbent upon quasi-pastors to take a census and to keep a spiritual status register.[41] Though in strict terminology they are not pastors, quasi-pastors nevertheless have the same rights and duties as canonical pastors have, and any ruling made for pastors applies also to them.[42]

Also among those having parochial power must included military chaplains.[43] Since the chaplain has the principal care of the

[41] Just as dioceses are dividend into parishes, so prefectures apostolic and vicariates apostolic are divided into quasi-parishes. The rectors who have charge of the quasi-parishes are called quasi-pastors. Cf. canon 216 § 1 and § 3.

[42] Canon 451.

[43] S. C. Consist., 8 dec. 1939 — *AAS*, XXXI (1939), 710.

souls of those who live on the military reservation, he ought, as best he can, to take a regular census and keep a spiritual status register. The expression, "as best he can," is used for it is very often impossible, what with the constant change of personnel within our modern army camps, to keep any kind of an accurate account of the souls entrusted to his care. Yet those with some sort of stability (prudently forseen as remaining at the base for a year or more) should be accounted for in his records.

Rectors of seminaries, though not possessing the rights of a pastor in regard to the hearing of confessions and assistance at marriage, nevertheless enjoy full parochial jurisdiction in all other matters.[44] As such they are obliged to take a census and to keep a register. However because of the nature of the people involved and the close contact rectors have with those under their care it is easy to see the possibility of omitting a formal census. Nevertheless they are to keep a special spiritual status register in accord with the rules given by the Sacred Congregation of Seminaries and Universities.

Thus it has been seen that the assembling of the census and the keeping of the parochial spiritual status register are primarily the obligations of the pastor and and of those in law equal to pastors.

b) By way of vicarious agency

Augustine, pointed out that, although the obligation of keeping the register is in and of itself a grave one for the pastor, it is not strictly a personal obligation.[45] That is to say that the pastor may employ others to care for the register. The same is true in regard to the census.[46] What part, therfore, does the assistant or the curate have in these affairs?

The assistant does not possess all the rights and duties of the pastor's office. His privileges and obligations are determined by the diocesan statues, by his letter of appointment, by some other letter of the ordinary, or by the will of the pastor himself.[47] In accord with the common law the assistant is wihout any right or duty in regard to the parochial spiritual status register or the census.[48] This

44 Canons 891 and 1368.

45 *Commentary,* VII, 465.

46 *Digest,* II, 150.

47 Canon 476 § 6.

48 Augustine, *Commentary,* VII, 257; Chelodi, *De Personis,* n. 232.

follows naturally from the assumption that a curate is not the incumbent of a strict ecclesiastical office. The preponderance of opinion seems to favor his having only delegated powers,[49] hence, no office. De Meester[50] explicity declares that it belongs to the pastor to make the inscriptions in the spiritual status register. He adds, however, that the care of such matters is usually handed over to the curate. In an instruction concerning the parish census the Holy See not only acknowledges this fact but urges assistants to look upon the taking of a census as a part of their apostolic work, and thus to give themselves to it with zeal and devotion.[51] However, this does not constitute for assistants or curates a primary obligation. It remains for the pastor, to whom the care of souls is given in accord with the common law, to delegate this work to the assistant. The Holy See intended, as is evident from the context of its statement, to stress the notion that the priests of the parish rather than the laity should perform this duty.

It is true that in some dioceses invaluable aid to pastors in census-taking has been given by helpers, especially trained for the task, as well as by members of parochial organizations working under the supervision of the parish priest. It must be clearly understood, however, that the takng of the census by others than priests is but a preparation for the visit of the pastor or his assistant, and can never take its place.[52] Nevertheless these helpers can prepare the faithful to attach greater importance to the visit of the parish priest; they oftentimes smooth the way in difficult circumstances so that parishioners will welcome the priest and profit spiritually by his visit.

If a parish is so large, or the parishioners are so numerous, as to make it impossible for the parish clergy to take up the census personally, the pastor should avail himself of the service of such helpers who are qualified to co-operate with him in this work.[53] The choice

[49] Bastnagel, *The Appointment of Parochial Adjutants and Assistants,* p. 144.

[50] *Iuris Canonici, et Iuris Canonico — Civilis Compendium* (nova ed., 3 vols. in 4, Brugis, 1921-28) II, n. 887.

[51] *Digest,* II 150.

[52] Loc. cit.

[53] *Loc. cit.*

then lies between the religious and the laity.

Obviously, the laity is the least well equipped for the taking of a census. The fact that the census often involves the disclosure of matters of conscience is a handicap. Respondents are more prone to conceal important facts from lay enumerators. Furthermore no pastor should want any of his lay people to be the repositories or the dispensers of intimate details in the lives of his parishioners. There is a great risk of gossip, if not scandal. In spite of these objections, however, an imperfect census assembled by the laity is better than no census at all. Very often the lay members of the St. Vincent de Paul Societies and of the Legions of Mary do excellent work minus any of the harmful effects just explained. The laity, however, should not be employed unless it is absolutely necessary.[54]

The main advantage in the use of religious is the fact that they are skilled in census-taking and, what is more, devote full time to visiting the families in the parish. Futhermore, many fallen-away Catholics refuse to see a priest until they have been prepared, kindly and tactfully, as only the religious can do during several calls. Yet such religious are still few in number, and even they cannot aspire to the performance of certain functions that must await the later visitations undertaken by priests.

Census work is part of the priest's "ministry of the word." It is a right which he cannot abdicate, an obligation which he cannot allow others to usurp. Census work belongs essentially to the priest. It is an important priestly function, and may not be delegated to others needlessly.[55] There has been a mistaken tendency to turn over the complete task of parish visitations to women religious or Sisters. This tendency must be resisted, since it nullifies one of the main purposes of the census, viz., bringing the parish priest into direct contact with his people. The danger is ever present that individual Catholic families will become merely names on an index card. It is one thing to note an invalid marriage on a census card, but quite

[54] C. Nuesse-T. Harte, *The Sociology of the Parish,* p. 241; cf. O'-Brien's article on San Diego convert work — *AER,* May 1953.

[55] O'Grady, "The Parish Census," *ER,* LXXX (1929), 42; Pius XI, litt. encycl. *Ad catholici sacerdotii,* 20 dec. (1935), *AAS, XXVIII* (1936), 15.

another thing to remember the faces of those who are invalidly married

Some bishops have begun the practice of having seminarians assist the parish priest during the summer months in this essential work.[56] This practice has many advantages, both for the seminarian and for the priest, which far outweigh any possible disadvantages. For the seminarian it affords an opportunity to put into practice the learning he has received in the seminary classroom; it helps him to evaluate the main problems with which he will be confronted after his ordination, and hence, gives him an incentive to learn more of them upon his return to the seminary. Not to be overlooked is the fact that it will instill in him a realization of the importance and the need of census work in his priestly life, and an understanding of the best methods to be employed.

For the parish priest the use of seminarians affords the groundwork for his own later vistation. It brings to his attention cases and situations whch demand his immediate care. In large, sprawling parishes it enables him to learn firsthand of people who might otherwise be overlooked because of his other heavy duties or his lack of time. It is for him as valuable a help as that which could be given by women religious or Sisters under the same conditons. But, as with them, the seminarian can never adequately take the priest's place. His own visit on what may be called "follow-up" work is always necessary.

Article IV: The Time at which the Obligation Binds

a) The parish census

No strict time limit in which a parish census must be taken becomes determinable in a general work of this sort. The Holy See has left it to the individual local ordinaries to determine the time according to the conditions which prevail in their respective dioceses.[57] However, it should be "current" and taken at "regular intervals."[58]

[56] Shaughnessy, "Catholic Statistics and the *Status Animarum* Record," *ER,* C (1939), 97.

[57] *Digest,* II, 149.

Berengo reflected a similar position as early as 1877, when he taught that the pastor must visit his parishioners often in order to have a "continuous" record of the spiritual status of the people living within the parish. It was a task, as he phrased it, "to be undertaken without delay."[59] Peterson, some 50 years later, in writing on the parish census, likewise called for a "regularly" conducted census.[60] The time, in a later article by Shaughnessy, was made more specfic. He advocated a continuous, "yearly" census on the part of each pastor.[61]

There was nothing new in this suggestion. Many decades earlier there had appeared a pastoral manual in which it was proposed that the pastor associate the taking of the census with the yearly blessing of the homes of his parishioners. According to the translator of this work it was evident that "the author regarded the blessing as a means to an end; and the end is that the parish priest should, in the course of his visits to the different houses, acquire a thorough knowledge of his parishioners, and of their spiritual and temporal wants . . . knowledge which every parish priest is bound to acquire in virtue of a divine precept."[62]

b) The parochial spiritual status register

Like the census, the time in which the parochial spiritual status must be renewed is to be determined by the statutes of each diocese or by the prescriptions of the local ordinary, most of whom at present require the renewal at least every five years.[63] Monacelli (1715) long ago held that the register should be renewed if possible each year, or at least within every three year period;[64] now in our

[58] *Digest,* II, 147 and 149.

[59] *Enchiridion Parochorum, seu Institutiones Theologiae Pastoralis* (2. ed., Venetiis: Ex Typographia Aemiliana, 1877), p. 449, n. 214.

[60] "Knowing our Own," *ER,* LXXXIII (1933), 291.

[61] "Catholic Statistics and the *Status Animarum* Record," *ER,* C (1939), 97.

[62] Frassinetti-Hutch, *The New Parish Priests' Practical Manual* p. 134. The original Italian edition had appeared in Novara in 1863.

[63] Murphy, "Parish Records," *ER,* LXV (1929), 12.

[64] *Formularium Legale Practicum Fori Ecclesiastici* . (3. Romana ed., cum supplemento novissimo, 4 vols. in 3, Romae: Ex typographia Reverendae Camerae Apostolicae, 1844), Tom. I, tit. X, n. 1, p. 286 (hereafter cited *Formularium Fori Ecclesiastici*)

own day Fanfani among other authors recommend a yearly revision.[65] In any case the parochial spiritual status register should be kept up-to-date. Recent births should be noted at once, new parishioners should be inscribed without delay, and the names of those who leave the parish cancelled out the moment this fact becomes known to the pastor.[66]

The importance of taking a continuous census and of keeping an up-to-date parochial spiritual status register cannot be minimized. If the recording of items is to be fully effective and is to accomplish the purpose for which it is intended, then the items must be current factors. Conditions which existed in years previous may be completely changed. New families may have entered the parish, new-born children may need baptism, homes may have been broken by separation or divorce, invalid marriages may have taken place, marriages once incapable of validation may now be workable. These the pastor must diligently inquire about if he is to carry out a successful parochial program adapted to an alleviation of the existing needs.

[65] *De Iure Parochorum*, p. 71.

[66] Barbosa, *Pastoralis Sollicitudo*, Pars I, Cap. VIII, p. 23.

CHAPTER IX

THE MANNER OF TAKING THE CENSUS AND OF KEEPING THE PAROCHIAL SPIRITUAL STATUS REGISTER

ARTICLE I: THE CENSUS

a) Preparations

Nothing is to be found in the law concerning the manner in which the census is to be taken. What follows is the result of a survey of many pastoral manuals and articles which have been written on the subject. It is the pastor, working under the guidance of his proper ordinary, who must choose the method and means best suited for his locality. Sometimes it will be impossible for him personally to take the census. At other times he may require outside help in his own survey. However, a general norm of action which can be adapted by each pastor to local conditions will herein be presented and, insofar as it is possible, be evaluated.

Before the actual census begins, certain preliminary work must be done by the pastor.[1] For this he ought to secure a map of his parish either from a real estate agency, a city bureau, or the chamber of commerce. Rural pastors may find county atlases or rural-delivery maps, available from the United States Postmaster General, quite helpful. This parish map should record the residential areas to be surveyed, as well as the presence of parks and business houses, and furnish other similar information.

A decision must then be made regarding the plan for contacting the people living in the parish. This must be based upon the pastor's ability to take the census, and with due consideration for the size of the parish. Should conditions be such that he himself will be unable to devote his own time to the work, whether because of ill health or other pressing duties that require his attention, then he must determine whom he will delegate as enumerators. There is little if any problem if the pastor has assistants assigned to his parish. They, of course, are ideal enumerators for the parish census is es-

[1] C. Nuesse — T. Harte, *The Sociology of the Parish*, p. 252.

sentially the work of a priest.[2] If such priests be too few in number, then the pastor could arrange to have a religious group, e.g., the Mission Helpers of the Sacred Heart, or a parish society, e.g., the St. Vincent de Paul Society or the Legion of Mary, or even a select group of his parishioners, assist him in the work of census-taking.

Every home in the parish must be visited for only through a visitation of all the homes may the pastor feel assured that all Catholics, be they good, bad or indifferent, are accounted for.[3] Never should he feel content to visit only those families whom he or his enumerators know to be good practicing Catholics.

Particular difficulty must be faced in those localities wherein the members of a national parish intermingle with the members of the territorial parish. It is true that each pastor has his own rights as to his own parishioners. However, the problem arises from the parishioners themselves. Very often lax Catholics who do not want to speak with their own priest will tell any enumerator who happens to be conducting the census that they belong to the "other" parish. Since most of these people are reluctant to supply all the information required on the census questionnaire, the only solution seems that of having the enumerator record simply their name and address, which his pastor will then send to their "acknowledged" proper pastor. The acknowledged pastor in turn ought to check his parochial spiritual status register and, should the entry be lacking, visit said family and supply for the deficiency. By such mutual co-operation every soul will eventually be accounted for.[4]

The parish should then be divided by the pastor into sections based upon the density of the population and the area covered by the parish. No section should be so large that it cannot be covered by one person in a week. Should the laity be employed as enumerators, they would best be assigned to sections of the parish which are familiar to them. Despite their personal knowledge of the territory and its residents it would be well to warn them that all homes must be visited.[5]

[2] *Digest,* II, 150.

[3] "Studies and Conferences," *ER,* LIII (1915), 693; *supra,* p. 116.

[4] Cf. Francis "The Dying National Parish and Compulsory Membership Registration," *ER,* LXXXXV (1936), 381.

[5] C. Nuesse — T. Harte, *The Sociology of the Parish,* p. 253.

b) Methods used in contacting the parishioners.

Because of the danger of scandal and in consequence of the reluctance of the faithful to explain their difficulties to a layman, the pastor, when by circumstances constrained to employ the laity as his delegates, ought to do one of two things. He will either have his parish enumerators ask only for general information, e.g., the name, address, religion (whether they once were Catholics or are interested in the Catholic religion), telephone number, and the time suggested for the visitation of the priest, in which case he himself or one of his assistants must later return;[6] or he may, as is often done today in the so called 48 hour census, have his enumerators deliver in person to each family that acknowledges membership in the Catholic Church a complete census card along with the request to have it ready in a sealed envelope the following day, when the enumerator will return to collect it in order to bring it to the rectory. This, of course, is not ordinarily a desirable method, since it leaves open the possibility of false or evasive answers, given oftentimes with a view to not meeting the priest, and it defeats one of the main purposes of the census—contact between the priest and his flock. In such a census the danger that these people will remain to the pastor as names on a card is great. Nevertheless such a census is better than none at all.

Perhaps even worse is the system one sometimes sees employed today. That system involves the distribution of census cards, either through the mail or at the door of the church, with the request that it be returned in a completed form to the rectory. Not only is such a census open to all the criticism noted above, but even more seriously it fails to account for the non-practicing, fallen-away Catholic. Certainly those who fail to attend church are the ones who should be contacted, even more so than those who are faithful to their religious obligations. This system then should be abolished. There is no justification for it, since it fails to achieve the most important purpose for which the census is intended.

The ideal census, of course, is that which is taken by the pastor in conjunction with his priest assistants by means of a house to house visitation.[7] Sometimes a division of the labor proves advantageous,

[6] Navagh, *The Apostolic Parish*, p. 35.

[7] Gavisk, "The Census of Catholics," *ER*, LIII (1915), 353.

one priest doing the visitaton, another the validation of marriages, and the third the instruction of converts. Again, it may prove to greater advantage either to have all the priests of the parish simultaneously go out on the census, or to have the work assigned to one priest who will be occupied with it all year around. It is for the pastor to decide on whatever system appears preferable. At this point it is well to note that care should be taken by all involved to avoid the old and damnable practice of asking for or accepting a money fee during the performance of this truly apostolic work.[8]

When the division of labor is determined, the assigned priest will begin his visitation of all the families in each section by going from door to door. Unless the laity has been employed to do the groundwork, i.e., to ascertain who are the Catholic residents or which residents are interested in the Catholic Church, and at what time they wish to receive the priest, the priest enumerator should not omit visiting any of the homes or apartments.

c) Practical suggestions

Practical suggestions on the manner in which the priest should conduct himself once he has started upon the census are found in abundance.[9] For the sake of completeness a summary of that procedure is here presented.

When approaching the front door the enumerator should never carry census cards, pamphlets, etc., where they will be in evidence. When the door is opened he may begin by giving the purpose of the visit and an explanation of the census. Then with care and prudence he ought to seek general information. Such questions as: "Are you a Catholic? Are there any Catholics living here? Are there any who ought to be Catholics? Have you any Catholic relatives?" and, finally, "Is there anyone living here who is interested in the Catholic Church?" are essential. Of course it is better not to ask these questions abruptly; one should introduce them naturally as part of the

[8] Shaughnessy, "Catholic Statistics and the *Status Animarum* Record," *ER*, C (1939), 98.

[9] Navagh, *The Apostolic Parish*, pp. 36 ff.; C. Nuesse — T. Harte, *The Sociology of the Parish*, pp. 254 ff.; Beehan, "The Priest and the Census," *ER*, CXIII (1935), 481 ff.; Berardi, *Compendium de Parocho*, n. 584; Frassinetti — Hutch, p. 134.

conversation. If the persons interviewed prove to be non-Catholic, the priest will wisely refrain from writing anything down in their presence. These first few minutes are important. On the impression the priest creates when he enters the home depends the success of his whole visit.

If the visited home is composed of Catholics, the priest should observe whether any indication of real faith are evident.[10] This can be ascertained from the manner in which he is received, from the presence of holy pictures, crucifixs, or statues as Christian ornaments in the home. If he be greeted with an embarassing silence or only with reluctance, he must first attempt to break down the opposition by means of a casual and friendly conversation. In doing so he probably will discover the reason for the respondent's prejudice, so that in a few minutes[11] (the visitation of a home should never be unduly prolonged) he may gain the necessary friendly atmosphere in which he will seek to ask the questons incorporated on the census card. If a particular respondent proves difficult, it may be best to interrupt the visit at an early stage. Sometimes it will take two or three visits. Rarely should the priest censure the respondent or any member of the family. He should do so only when it is absolutely necessary, and always in a tactful manner.

Once the anti-clerical prejudice has been removed, the priest is ready to ask for the information sought on the census card. He must not feel that his queries should be limited to these particular questions as a maximum, though as a minimum they ought never to be omitted. It is his right to ask any questions that will enable him to attain the purpose for which the census is intended. Correlatively, it is the duty of the respondent to answer to the best of his ability. Very often the additionally evoked information proves to be of considerable value. In any case the questioning should be informal. When the priest is about to depart, he may well leave some interesting and helpful pamphlet, and particularly show himself thankful to the respondent for the time and co-operation he has received.

[10] Berardi, *Compendium de Parocho*, n. 584.

[11] Navagh, *The Apostolic Parish*, p. 38: "The visit should be short

d) "Follow-up" work

Once the census has been completed, the real work is about to begin. The acquired information must be placed in the parochial spiritual status register, and the essential "follow-up" work started. This work may be classified under seven main projects:[12]

1) validating marriages;
2) arranging for the baptism of the unbaptized and the confirmation of the ones not yet confirmed;
3) visiting the fallen-away Catholics discovered in the census with a view to bringing them back to the Church;
4) visiting the homes of children not attending the Catholic school in order to arrange for their entrance; or at least for their attendance at religious instruction classes;
5) visiting the homes of children attending religious instruction classes in order to persuade their parents to send them to the Catholic school;
6) visiting those who have shown an interest in the Catholic Church with the endeavor to deepen interest in the Church in order to persuade them to attend religious instruction classes.

To this list could be added such items as the repeated sympathetic visiting of the weak members of the parish in order to persuade them to frequent the sacraments and to attend Mass, the restoration of peace among those who have been at emnity with one another, and the bestowal of help on those who are in need, whether it be spiritual or temporal. The poor, the widows, the orphans, the wards, the sick and the aged, all should receive special attention.[13]

In order to keep effective the census when once completed and to keep informed, it is advisable that the pastor appoint certain members of his parish to be on the lookout for new families moving into the parish. Changes can thus be reported to him at once, and accordingly he will be able to visit incoming familes without delay.[14]

and businesslike."

12 Navagh, *The Apostolic Parish*, p. 39.

13 *Barbosa, Pastoralis Sollicitudo*, Pars 1, Cap. VII, p. 23; Giraldi, Pars I, Cap. VII, p. 65.

14 Navagh, *The Apostolic Parish*, p. 41

The task of taking a census and of following up the leads which the census has provided is not an easy one. This work, even when efficiently executed, will not cure all the evils of the parish, nor will it reclaim all the erring souls. Unfavorable conditions, as reflected in large city parishes with an ever shifting element in the population, or in rural parishes with an insufficient number of priests for the large areas covered, not to speak of the conditions of a moral nature, make the work difficult. Yet the Holy See warns that "these difficulties do not justify the parish priest in neglecting the means which, as experience shows, enable him to double or treble the fruits of his pastoral labors."[15]

Article II: The Parochial Spiritual Status Register

It has been seen that the pastor, by virtue of his office, is the one who has the care of the parochial spiritual status register, that he is to frequently renew it, (the exact time depending upon diocesan statutes of the prescription of the local ordinary) and that he need not send a yearly copy of it to the episcopal curia.[16] Now the question arises as to whether it is necessary that the register be a bound note-book or tablet or may the practice now in vogue of using catalogued index cards be continued.

a) Book or Index

The Code prescribes that the parochial registers be parochial books,[17] that is, not a mere collection of loose-leaf papers or certificates. Moreover, since these books are dedicated to the purpose of registering the official ecclesiastical acts from which each one draws its name[18] in accordance with the prescriptions of the *Roman Ritual* and the Code, many authors require that they be of good quality linen paper, well-bound, and that they contain an ample index.[19] The purpose of such regulations, of course, is to avoid the possibility of fraud, loss, disorder, etc. Many other commentators,

[15] *Digest,* II, 148.
[16] Canon 470, § 3;
[17] Canon 470, § 1.
[18] Monacelli, *Formularium Fori Ecclesiastici,* Tom. I, tit. X, n. 2, p. 286.
[19] O'Rourke, *Parish Registers,* p. 8.

however, make allowance for the frequent additions and changes that must be made in the parochial spiritual status register. For that register alone do they make exception and permit the use of index cards in a file instead of a regular book.[20]

From a practical point of view the latter is a very helpful suggestion and well within the bounds of canonical regulation, since a great deal of latitude is given in the matter of this unusual register.[21] Through the use of a file of index cards, in which each family is allotted one card, the names of new families can easily be inserted while the alphabetical order is being retained. Moreover, the records of the families which transfer to another parish can easily be removed. Erasures and striking out of recorded facts as new information is acquired can be kept to a minimum by simply removing the old card and inserting a new card with the correct information.

What is to be done with such records when once they are removed is a moot question. Berengo recommended the pastor's retaining of these records in another file for the eventuality that an inquiry be made concerning the stay of these families in his parish.[22] Others suggest that the record be sent on to the parish to which the family has moved, so that their new pastor will become familiar with their spiritual status.

The obvious solution is the original pastor's retention of the record. There is no advantage to be gained by spontaneously influencing the new pastor's appreciation of the incoming family by transmitting information which in a great part is subjective and sometimes prejudicial. If, however, the new pastor actually makes inquiry of the original pastor on some point or other regarding the family, a reply ought to be forthcoming, but the information contained therein should be confined to a factual accounting and not include personal opinions or evaluations. The practice of giving prejudical information can expose the information to libelous utterances. When a family has changed its parochial residence the

[20] Fanfani, *De Iure Parochorum*, p. 71; Berengo, *Enchiridion Parochorum*, p. 450, n. 214.

[21] Fanfani, *op. cit.*, p. 71.

[22] *Loc. cit.*

former pastor may, of course, notify the new pastor regarding this change.[23] In fact, it would help matters if such were a common practice among the shepherds of souls.

For the sake of easy reference it is suggested that variously colored cards or colored tabs on cards, raised above general level to be seen easily, be used. White cards could be used for outstanding and average Catholic families, yellow cards for those who are weak in their faith, and pink cards for those families which require the priest's immediate attention, e.g., when marriages are to be validated, when children are to be transferred to the Catholic school, when interested non-Catholics are to be given instructions, etc.[24] These cards, arranged in alphabetical order according to the first letter of the family name, should be kept in a strong metal file-cabinet for safe-keeping.

b) Inscription

The inscriptions upon these cards ought to be made in a readily legible fashion and in a logically successive order.[25] Ink that is guaranteed not to fade should be used rather than a lead pencil, since whatever is written by lead pencil will eventually blur and become indistinct.[26] The writing need not be in the pastor's own hand. Unlike the other registers which are to serve the purpose of documentary proof, the purpose of the parochial spiritual status register is of such a general character that the information may be typed in if the pastor so desires. Moreover, his signature is not needed on each card. As regards corrections, the pastor may repeatedly undertake them, and in fact should do so. It is a register to be kept as accurate and up-to-date as possible.

Concerning the language to be used most of the authors say nothing. Cappello in mentioning the point declares that it remains for the ordinary's prescription, the custom of the diocese, or synodal law to regulate this matter.[27] Latin, or perhaps some sort of symbol,

[23] O'Rourke, *Parish Registers,* p. 91.

[24] Peterson, "Knowing Our Own," *ER,* LXXXIII (1933), 291.

[25] Stang, *Pastoral Theology* (2. ed., New York, 1897), p. 310; Giraldi, Pars. I, Cap. VII, p. 64, n. 19.

[26] O'Rourke, *Parish Registers,* p. 9.

[27] *Tractatus Canonico-Moralis de Sacramentis* (5 vols., Vol. I, 5. ed., Romae: Marietti, 1947), I, 142, 139.

should be employed whenever the matter to be entered might offer occasion for scandal if it were read by others than the proper persons.[28] The *Roman Ritual* itself proposes the use of various signs to indicate the reception of the sacraments.[29] In earlier rituals, such as that of Paul V, quite an extensive system was employed. Today, however, the minimum is employed. "B," or a simple check mark under the column allotted to baptism, or, better still, the place of baptism noted in such a column, would suffice to indicate that baptism had been received. "C," or a check mark, may be used to indicate first Holy Communion, "Chr," or a check mark, for confirmation, etc.

c) Custody

Since the parochial spiritual status register contains information of a private nature, and yet is necessary for reference, it must be guarded accordingly. The Code, therefore, cautions the pastor to be diligent in this matter and, to insure the proper custody, requires its storage in the parochial archives.[30] The archives need not be a pretentious affair. For example, the rectory safe may well be used as the place for the keeping of this register,[31] but in any case it should always be under lock and key.[32] These archives, moreover, ought to be in a dry place, yet safely removed from any excessive heat. Hence they should not be placed near a fireplace, stove, or radiator.[33] It is not enough that the parish priest guard this register from fraudulent treatment at the hands of men; he must likewise take every precaution to preserve it from accident.

Since the parochial spiritual status register is of a secret nature, the pastor is not allowed to permit the laity to take it from the archives, or even to inspect it.[34] The Code itself cautions the pastor to be careful lest this register come into the hands of extraneous

[28] O'Rourke, *Parish Registers*, p. 9.

[29] *Rituale Romanum Pii Papae XI ad Normam Codicis Iuris Canonici Accomodatum* (Romae, 1925) VI, p. 364.

[30] Canon 470, § 4.

[31] O'Rourke, *Parish Registers*, p. 10.

[32] Van Espen, *Ius Ecclesiasticum Universum* (2 tomes, Lovanii, 1753), Pars I, tit. 5, cap. 5, p. 33; Aichner, *Compendium Iuris Ecclesiastici*, p. 433; Wernz — Vidal, *Ius Canonicum*, II, n. 737.

[33] Frassinetti — Hutch, p. 246.

[34] Canon 384, §1.

persons. This caution precludes the practice of allowing it to lie in open view where domestics and other persons may have ready access to it.[35]

Finally, it should be noted that no certificate as drawn from this register is to be issued, but a notification may be sent by the former pastor to the new pastor in the case of a family changing parishes.[36]

[35] Augustine, *Commentary,* II, 555; Frassinetti-Hutch, p. 247.
[36] O'Rourke, *Parish Registers,* p. 91.

CONCLUSIONS

1) The parish census and the parochial spiritual status register are distinct entities, the former being the means to be used for the obtaining of such information as belongs in the register. (p. 5)

2) In the earliest days of the Church the "diptychs of the living," at least by way of a resemblance, foreshadowed the present parochial spiritual status register. (pp. 14-16)

3) Only particular legislation was enacted in regard to the census and the parochial spiritual status register up to the beginning of the 17th century. This dealt mainly with such notions as who were to be included in the census and register, who were obliged to take the census and keep the register, how was it to be done, and what was to be done with this information once it was noted in the register. (p. 21 & 35)

4) *The Roman Ritual* of Paul V in 1614 afforded the first general legislation in regard to the parochial spiritual status register. There it is that one finds the information which is to be contained in the register and the form which is to be used in its inscription. (pp. 36-39)

5) Since nothing was added or changed by the common law in the period between the Ritual and the Code, and since canon 470, §1, is practically a restatement of the Ritual of Paul V, the commentaries written on this phase of the Ritual still apply. (p. 45)

6) The information to be sought for the parochial spiritual status register need not be limited to the matters that receive mention in the Roman Ritual. The pastor has a right and duty to inquire on all subjects which have a bearing on the respondent's social spiritual status. Hence he may ask such questions as pertain to the subjects education and economic status, and record the given answers in the register. (pp. 45-54)

7) Besides the regular parishioners (those having a domicile or a quasi-domicile in a parish), *vagi* are also to be numbered among the persons to be listed in the pastor's spiritual status register. Excluded are *peregrini*, religious, non-Catholics, and those who live in seminaries or on military reservations with no other domicile or

quasi-domicile. Members of national or of personal parishes are to be registered by their own proper pastor. (p. 66)

8) The obligation to take the census and to keep the register is a grave one. It rests upon the pastor and upon those who by law are accorded a status equivalent to a pastor's. This work may, in consequence of necessity, be delegated to others, preferably to the clergy. The time within which this work is to be done depends upon the prescriptions of the ordinary ,the demands made by local custom, or the ordinances of the diocesan statutes. In any case the census and the register must exist as a current and up-to-date record. (pp. 67 & 81)

9) The local ordinary may prescribe the matter to be included in the census and the register, and he may even prescribe the manner in which it is to be taken and kept; but he may not deprive the pastor of his parochial right to take the census and to keep the register as long as the pastor is at the same time faithfully fulfilling his duty. Failure of the pastor in the fulfillment of either of these obligations may result in his being subjected to a canonical penalty, even to the deprivation of his office, determinable by the ordinary when serious harm has been done. (pp. 68-70)

10) The parochial spiritual status register is to be shown to the local ordinary at the time of his visitation. However, a copy need not be sent to the episcopal curia each year, as it is to be done with reference to the other parochial registers. (pp. 70-71)

11) Various methods may be employed in the assembling of the parish census. The ideal census is one that is taken by the priests of the parish by means of a house to house visitation. Condemned is the practice of conducting the census by leaving census cards in the rear of the church, or by sending them through the mail with the request that they be filled in and returned to the rectory. (pp. 86-87)

12) The census and the parochial spiritual status register reflect their full potential value in the essential "follow-up" work by which marriages are validated, children are given catechetical instructions, weak Catholics are made strong in their faith, and non-Catholics are instructed in the Christian doctrine. (pp. 89-90)

13) Index cards, properly filed in alphabetical order, may be used in place of the ordinary bound book for the parochial spiritual

status register. The use of various colored cards is recommended for easy reference. (pp. 90-91)

14) The insriptions upon each card need not be in the pastor's own handwriting; they may in fact be typewritten. (p. 92)

15) These cards are to be kept in the parish archives. Care must be taken against their accidental destruction or their falling into the hands of extraneous persons. (p. 93)

16) When a family moves to another parish, then not a copy of the family's card but a simple notification of the change of parish, should be forwarded to the new pastor. (pp. 91 & 94)

BIBLIOGRAPHY

Sources

Acta Apostolicae Sedis, Commentarium Officiale, Romae, 1909—

Acta Ecclesiae Mediolanensis (*AEM*), a Sancto Carolo Cardinali S. Praxedis Archiep. condita, Frederici Cardinalis Borromaei Archiepiscopi Mediolani jussu collecta et edita, 2 tomi, Lugduni: Ex Officina Avissoniana et Joan. Posuet, 1682-1683.

Acta et Decreta Concilii Plenarii Baltimorensis III (1884), Baltimore, John Murphy 1886.

Acta et Decreta Concilii Provincialis Neo Eboracensis IV (1883), Neo Eboraci: Typis Societatis pro Libris Catholicis Evulgandis, 1886.

Acta et Decreta Sacrorum Conciliorum Recentiorum, Collectio Lacensis, 7 vols., Friburgi Brisgoviae: Sumptibus Herder, 1870-1892.

Acta et Decreta Synodi Plenariae Episcoporum Hiberniae Habitae aupd Maynutiam (1875), Dublini: Typis Browne et Nolan, 1877.

Canon Law Digest, The, 2 vols. and Supplement through 1948, Milwaukee: The Bruce Publishing Co., 1934, 1943, 1949.

Codex Iuris Canonici Pii X Pontificis Maximi iussu digestus, Benedicti Papae XV auctoritate promulgatus, Romae, 1917, and Westminister, Maryland: The Newman Book Shop, 1942.

Codex Theodosiani cum Constitutionibus Sermondianis, ediderunt adsumpto apparatu P. Kruger, Th. Mommsen, Berolini: apud Weidmannos, 1905.

Codicis Iuris Canonici Fontes cura Emi Petri Card. Gasparri editi, 9 vols., Romae (Postea Civitate Vaticana) : Typis Polyglottis Vaticanis, 1923-1939 (Vols. VII-IX ed. cura et studio Emi Iustiniani Card. Serédi).

Concilia Germaniae, Joannis Mauritii sumptu, Joannes Fredericus Schannat collegit et P. Josephus Hartzheim auxit et continuavit, 11 vols., Coloniae Augustae Agrippinensium: Typo viduae Joan. Wilhelmi Krakamp, et haeredum Christiani Simonis Bibliopolarum, 1759-1790.

Consilia Provincialia Baltimori (editio alter), Baltimore: John Murphy & Associates, 1851.

Corpus Iuris Canonici, Pars II, *Decretalium Collectiones,* ed Lipsiensis secunda, post Aemilii Ludvici Richteri curas. . . . instruxit Aemilius Friedberg, Lipsiae, 1881.

Corpus Scriptorum Ecclesiasticorum Latinorum, 71 vols., incomplete, Vindobonae, 1866—.

Decretales D. Gregorii Papae IX suae intergritati una cum glossis restitutae, Romae: in Aedibus Populi Romani, 1582.

Decretum Gratiani, emendatum et notationibus illustratum una cum glossis Gregorii XIII Pont. Max. iussu editum, 2 vols., Romae: in Aedibus Populi Romani, 1582.

Hardouin, Jean, *Acta Conciliorum et Epistolae Decretales ac Constitutiones Summorum Pontificum,* 12 vols., Pariis, 1714-1715.

Holy Bible, The, New York: The Douay Bible House, 1941.

Labbeus-Cossartius, *Sacrosancta Concilia,* 17 vols. in 18, Lutetiae Parisiorum, 1671-1672.

Liber Sextus Decretalium D. Bonifatii Papae VIII, suae integritati cum Clementinis et Extravagantibus, earumque Glossis restitutus, Romae: In Aedibus Populi Romani, 1582.

Mansi, J., *Sacrorum Conciliorum Nova et Amplissima Collectio,* 53 vols. in '60, Vols. 31b-53, Parisiis, Lepizig, Arnhem, 1901-1927. Vols. 1-31, Florentiae, Venetus, Parisiis, 1759-1798.

Monumenta Germaniae Historica edidit Societas Aperiendis Fontibus Rerum Germanicarum Medii Aevi, Libelli de Lite Imperatorum et Pontificum Saec. XI et XII Conscripta, 3 vols., ed. E. Sackur, Hannoverae, 1891-1892-1897.

Pallottini, Salvator, *Colletio conclusionum et resolutionum quae in causis propositis apud Sacram Congregationem Cardinalium S. Concilii Tridentini interpretum prodierunt ab eius institutione anno MDLXIV ad annum MDCCCLX, distinctis titulis alphabetico ordine per materias digesta,* 17 vols., Romae, 1868-1893.

Rituale Romanum Pii Papae XI ad Norman Codicis Iuris Canonici Accomodatum, Romae, 1925.

Rituale Romanum Pauli V Pont. Max. Jussu Editum, Romae: Typis et Sumptibus Philippi de Rubeis, 1652.

Schroeder, Henry, *Canons and Decrees of the Council of Trent,* St. Louis: B. Herder Book Co., 1941.

Thesaurus Resolutionum Sacrae Congregationis Concilii, 167 vols., Urbini, 1718-1741; Romae, 1741-1908

Reference Works

Abbo, J. — Hannan, J., *The Sacred Canons, A Concise Presentation of the Current Disciplinary Norms of the Church,* 2 vols., St. Louis: B. Herder Book Co., 1952.

A Catechism of Christian Doctrine, Revised Edition of the Baltimore Catechism No. 3, Paterson, N. J.: St. Anthony Guild Press, 1949.

Aertnys, J. — Damen, C., *Theologia Moralis secundum doctrinam S. Alfonsi De Ligorio Doct. Ecclesiae,* 16. ed., Roma: Marietti, 1950.

Aichner, Simon, *Compendium Iuris Ecclesiastici,* 6 ed., Brixinae, 1887.

Augustine, Charles , *A Commenary on the New Code of Canon Law,* 8 vols., St. Louis, Mo.: B. Herder Book Co., Vol. II, 3 ed., 1919, Vol. VII, 3. ed., 1930.

Ayrinhac, H. A., *Penal Legislation in the New Code of Canon Law,* Cincinnati: Benziger Brothers, 1920.

Barbosa, A.. *Pastoralis Sollicitudinis sive de Officio et Potestate Parochi Descriptio* (Quinta Edito prioribus emendatior, cum summariis et indicibus locupletissimis), Lugduni: Sumptibus Philippi Borde, Laurentii Arnaud, et Claudius Regaud, 1655.

Baruffaldus, Hieronymus, *Ad Rituale Romanum Commentaria,* 2 vols., Florentiae, 1847.

Bastnagel, Clement, *The Appointment of Parochial Adjutants and Assistants,* The Catholic University of America Canon Law Studies, n. 58, Washington, D. C.: The Catholic University of America Press, 1930.

Berardi, Aemilius, *Compendium de Parocho,* Faventiae: Ex Typographis Novelli, 1887.

Berengo, Joannes, *Enchiridion Parochorum seu Institutiones Theologiae Pastoralis,* 2. ed., Venetiis: Ex Typographia Aemiliana, 1877.

Beste, Udalricus, *Introductio in Codicem,* 2. ed., Collegeville, Minn: St. John's Abbey Press, 1944.

Blat, Albertus, *Commentarium Textus Codicis Iuris Canonici,* 5 vols. in 6, Romae: Ex typographia Pontificia in Instituto Pii X, 1919-1927.

Boehmer, Iustus, *Jus Parochiale,* Halae Magdeb.: Litteris et impensis Orphanotrophei, 1760.

Bona, Joannes, *Rerum Liturgicarum Libri Duo,* Taurini, 1747-1753.

Bouix, D., *Tractatus, de Parocho,* 3. ed., Parisiis, 1880.

Bouscaren, T. L. — Ellis, A., *Canon Law, A Text and Commentary,* Milwaukee: Bruce Publishing Co., 1948.

Cabrol, F. — Laclercq, H. — Marrou, H. I., *Dictionnaire d'Archéologie Chrcétienne et de Liturgie,* Paris, 1907—.

Cappello, Felix, *Summa Iuris Canonici,* 3 vols., Vol. 1, 5. ed., Romae: Typis Pontificiae Universitatis Gregorianae, 1951.

——— ———, *Tractatus Canonico — Moralis de Sacramentis,* 5 vols., Vol. I, 5. ed., Romae: Marietti, 1947.

Catholic Biblical Association, The, *A Commentary on the New Testament,* Kansas City: W. Sadlier, Inc., 1942.

Catholic Encyclopedia, The, 15 vols., Index and 2 supplements, New York, 1907-1922.

Cavalieri, J., *Opera Omnia Liturgica,* 5 vols., Venetiis, 1758.

Cavigioli, Giovanni, *Manuale di diritto canonico,* 3. ed., Torino: Societa Edritrice Internazionale, 1946.

Chelodi, I., *Ius de Personis iuxta Codicem Iuris Canonici,* Tridenti, 1922.

Ciesluk, Joseph, *National Parishes in the United States,* The Catholic University of America Canon Law Studies, n. 190, Washington, D. C.: The Catholic University of America Press, 1944.

Coogan, Thomas, *Catholic Fertility in Florida,* Washington, D. C.: The Catholic University of America Press, 1946.

Coronata, Matthaeus (Conte A.) *Institutiones Iuris Canonici ad Usam Utriusque Cleri et Scholarum,* 2 ed., 5 vols., Taurini: Marietti, 1939-1947.

Creusen, J., *Religious Men and Women in the Code,* 5 ed., Milwaukee-Bruce Publishing Co., 1940.

De Meester, A., *Iuris Canonici et Iuris Canonico — Civilis Compendium,* nova ed., 3 vols. in 4, Brugis, 1921-1928.

De Segusio, Henricus, *In Quinque Decretalium Commentaria,* 5 vols. in 3, Venetiis, 1581.

Devoti, J. *Institutionum Canonicarum Libri IV,* 4 vols., Leodii, 1860.

Duchesne, L. — McClure, M. L., *Christian Worship,* London, 1903.

Encyclopedia of the Social Sciences, New York: MacMillan Co., 1937—.

Enciclopedia Universal Illustrade, Barcelona: Hyon de J. Espasa, 1903—.

Fanfani, P., *De Iure Parochorum ad Norman Codicis Iuris Canonici,* Taurini — Romae: Marietti, 1924.

Feine, H. E., *Kirchliche Rechtsgeschichte, Die katholische Kirche,* Weimar: Hermann Bohlaus Nachfolger, 1950.

Ferrari, J. C., *Summa Institutionum Canonicarum,* 7. ed., Genuae, 1901.

Ferraris, L., *Prompta Bibliotheca Canonica, Iuridica, Moralis, Theologica necon Ascetia, Polemica, Rubristica, Historica,* 9 vols., Romae, 1885-1899.

Frassinetti, Joseph — Hutch, William, *The New Parish Priest's Practical Manual,* 2 ed., London and New York: Burns and Oates, 1885.

Funk, F. X. *Didascalia et Constitutiones Apostolorum,* 2 vols., Paderbornae, 1905.

Giraldi, Ubaldus, *Animadversiones et Additamenta ex Posterioribus Summorum Pontificum Constitutionibus et Sacrarum Congregationum De.cretis Desumpta ad Augustinum Barbosa, De Officio et Potestate Parochi,* Romae, 1774.

Hinschius, P., *Das Kirchenrecht der Katholiken und Protestanten in Deutschland,* 6 vols., Berlin, 1869-1897.

Kelly, Bernard, *The Functions Reserved to Pastors,* The Catholic Unicersity of America Canon Law Studies, n. 250, Washington, D. C.: The Catholic University of America Press, 1947.

Kelly, G., *Catholics and the Practice of Faith,* Washington, D. C.: The Catholic University of America Press, 1946.

Koudelka, C., *Pastors, Their Rights and Duties,* The Catholic University of America Canon Law Studies, n. 11, Washington, D. C.: The Catholic University of America, Press 1921.

Leage, R. W., *Roman Private Law,* 2. ed. by C. H. Ziegler; London: MacMillan and Company, 1930; Reprint, 1948.

Lundberg, *Social Research,* New York: Longmans, Green & Co., 1942.

Mabillon, J., *Acta Sanctorum Ordinis S. Benedicti, in Classes Saeculorum Distributa,* 9 vols., Venetiis, 1783.

Migne, J., *Patrologiae Cursus Completus, Series Graeca,* 161 vols., Parisiis, 1857-1866.

———, *Patrologiae Cursus Completus, Series Latina,* 221 vols., Parisiis, 1844-1855.

Monacelli, Franciscus, *Formularium Legale Practicum Fori Ecclesiastici,* edito tertia Romana cum supplemento novissimo, 4 vols. in 3, Romae: Ex Typographis Reverendae Camerae Apostolicae, 1844.

Mothon, Joseph, *Institutions Canoniques,* 3 vols., Parisiis, 1922-1924.

Navagh, J., *The Apostolic Parish,* New York: P. J. Kennedy & Sons, 1950.

Nuesse, C., — Harte, T., *The Sociology of the Parish,* Milwaukee: Bruce Publishing Co., 1951.

Ogg, F., — Ray P., *Introduction to American Government,* 9 ed., New York: Appleton-Century-Crofts, Inc., 1948.

O'Rourke, John, *Parish Registers,* The Catholic University of America Canon Law Studies, n. 88, Washington, D. C., The Catholic University of America Press, 1934.

Parsch, Pius — Eckhoff, Frederic C., *The Liturgy of the Mass,* St. Louis and London: B. Herder Book Co., 1936; reprint, 1942.

Poulet, Charles-Raemers, S. A., *A History of the Catholic Church,* translated from the 4. French edition, 2 vols., London: B. Herder Book Co., 1935-1936; reprint, 1948.

Pirhing, E., *Jus Canonicum in V Libris Decretalium,* 4 vols., Dilingae, 1722.

Reiffenstuel, Anacletus, *Jus Canonicum Universum,* 5 vols in 7, Parisiis, 1864-1870.

Rossi, J., *De Paroecia,* Romae: Pustet, 1923.

Schaefer, T. *De Religiosis ad Norman Iuris Canonici,* 4 ed., Roma: Editrice Apostolato Catholico, 1947.

Schaefer, Henerich, *Pfarrkirche und Stift im Deutschen Mitteralter,* Kirchenrechtiche Abhandlugen, hrsg. von U. Stutz, 3. Heft, Stuttgart, 1903.

Schnepp, G., *Leakage from a Catholic Parish,* Kirkwood, Mo.: Maryhurst Press, 1942.

Semeria, G. — Berry, E. S., *The Eucharist Liturgy in the Roman Rite,* Ratisbon: Pustet, 1911.

Shaughnessy, G., *Has the Immigrant Kept the Faith?*, New York: MacMillan Co., 1925.

Slafkosky, A. L., *The Canonical Episcopal Visitation of the Diocese,* The Catholic University of America Canon Law Studies, n. 142, Washington, D. C.: The Catholic University of America Press, 1941.

Smith, W. — Cheetham, S., *A. Dictionary of Christian Antiquities,* 2 vols., Hartford, 1880.

Stang, William, *Pastoral Theology,* 2 ed., New York: Benziger Bros., 1897.

Suarez, E., *De Remotione Parochorum* Romae: Scuola Tipografica Pii X, 1931.

Thomassinus, L., *Vetus et Nova Ecclesiae Disciplina,* 10 vols., Magontiaci, 1787.

Two Basic Social Encyclicals, New York: Benziger Brothers, 1943.

Van Espen, Z., *Jus Ecclesiasticum Universum,* 2 tomes, Lovanii, 1753.

Vermeersch, A., *Theologiae Moralis,* 4 vols., Vol., 111, 4 ed. Roma: Typ. Pontificiae Universitatis Gregoriannae, 1948.

Vermeersch, A. — Creusen, J., *Epitome Iuris Canonici,* 4 ed., 3 vols., Mechliniae — Romae: H. Dessain, 1929-1931.

Villien, A., *A History of the Commandments of the Church,* St. Louis, 1915.

Waldron, Joseph, *The Minister of Baptism,* The Catholic University of America Canon Law Studies, n. 170, Washington, D. C.: The Catholic University of America Press, 1942.

Webster's Collegiate Dictionary, 5 ed., Springfield, Mass: G. & C. Merriam Co., 1943.

Wernz, F., *Ius Decretalium,* 6 vols., Romae, 1898-1914, Vol. II, 3. ed., Prati 1915.

Wernz F. — Vidal, P., *Ius Canonicum,* 7 vols. in 8, Vol. I, 1938; Vol. II, 3 ed., a. P. Aguirre recognita, 1934; Vol III, 1933; Vol. IV, Pars I, 1934, pars 2, 1935; Vol. V, 3. ed., a. P. Aguirre recognita, 1946; Vol. VI, 1927; Vol. VII, 1937, Romae: Apud Aedes Universitatis Gregorianae.

Woywod, S., — Smith C., *A Practical Commentary on the Code of Canon Law,* New York: Joseph F. Wagner, Inc., 1948.

ARTICLES

Anon., "The Parish That Came Back," *The Ecclesiastical Review* LXI (1919), 27-37.

Beehan, T., "The Priest and the Census," *The Ecclesiastical Review,* CXIII 481-489.

Chose, S., "What the New Census Means," *Public Affairs Pamphlets,* No. 56.

Clemens, A. "The Need for Constructive Thinking in Sociological Research," *The American Catholic Sociological Review,* I (1940-), 75-78.

Foraneus, "Studies and Conferences," *The Ecclesiastical Review,* LIII (1914), 687-693.

Francis, H., "The Dying National Parish and Compulsory Membership Registration," *The Ecclesiastical Review,* LXXXXV (1936), 381-391.

Gavisk, F., "The Census of Catholics," *The Ecclesiastical Review,* LIII (1915-), 332-337.

Jedin, Hubert. "Konzil von Trient und Kirchenmatrikeln," *Zeitschrift der Savigny-Stiftung,* Kan. Abtlg., XXXII (1943), 419-494.

————, "La origine dei registri parrocchiali e il Concilio di Trento," *Il Concilio di Trento,* Anno II, n. 4 (1943), 323-336.

Larraona, A., "De Potestate Paroeciali Relate ad Religiosos", *Commentarium Pro Religiosis,* VIII (1927), 36-41.

Murphy, J., "Parish Records," *The Ecclesiastical Review,* LXV (1921), 1-12.

McGroarty, J., "Census Findings in a Negro Parish," *The Catholic World,* CLVI (1942), 325-339.

O'Grady, J., "The Parish Census" *The Ecclesiastical Review, LXXX* (1929), 30-42.

Peterson, J., "Knowing Our Own," *The Ecclesiastical Review, LXXXIII* (1933), 291-301.

Saegmüller, J. B., "Die Entstehung und Entwicklung ker Kirchenbücher im katholischen Deutschland bis zur Mitte der 18. Jahrhunderts," *Theologische Quartalschrift,* LXXXI (1899), 206-258.

Schnipp, J. "Nationality and Leakage," *The American Catholic Sociological Review,* III (1942), 154-163.

Shaughnessy, G., "Catholic Statistics and the *Status Animarum* Record," *The Ecclesiastical Review,* C (1939)), 97-108.

Periodicals

American Catholic Sociological Review, The, Chicago, Loyola University, 1940—.

American Ecclesiastical Review, The Vols. I-XXXII, Philadelphia, 1889-1905; from 1905: *The Ecclesiastical Review,* Vols. XXXIII-CIX, Philadelphia, 1905-1943; from 1944: *The American Ecclesiastical Review,* Washington, D. C., Vol. CX, 1944—.

Apollinaris, Romae, 1928—.

Commentarium pro Religiosis (later [1935], Commentarium pro Religiosis et Missionariis), Romae, 1920—.

Homiletic and Pastoral Review, The, New York, 1900—.

Il Concilio di Trento, Publicazione Trimestrale a Cura del Comitato per il IV Centenario del Concilio Trindentino — Curia Arcivescovile — Trento, Roma, 1943.

Theologische Quartalschrift, Rottenburg a. N., 1819—.

Zeitchrift der Savigny — Stiftung Kanonistische Abtelung, Weimar: Verlag Hermann Böhlaus Nachfolger, 1911—.

ABBREVIATIONS

AAS—*Acta Apostolicae Sedis*
AER—*The American Ecclesiastical Review*
AEM—*Acta Ecclesiae Mediolanensis*
ASS—*Acta Sanctae Sedis*
CSEL—*Corpus Scriptorum Ecclesiasticorum Latinorum*
Fontes—*Codicis Iuris Canonici Fontes*
MPG—Migne, *Patrologia Graeca*
MPL—Migne, *Patrologia Latina*
S. C. C.—*Sacra Congregatio Concilii*
S. C. de Prop Fide—*Sacra Congregatio de Propaganda Fide.*
TQS—*Theologische Quartalschrift*
ZSS—*Zeitschrift der Savigny — Stiftung*

ALPHABETICAL INDEX

BIOGRAPHICAL NOTE

William Francis Fitzgerald was born on January 21, 1926, in Newark, New Jersey. He received his elementary and high school education at St. Mary's Parochial School in South Amboy, New Jersey. In the fall of 1943 he entered St. Charles College, Catonsville, Maryland, where he received his Associate of Arts degree in June of 1945. His philosophical studies he made at Old St. Mary's, Paca Street, Baltimore, Maryland, where he obtained the Bachelor of Arts degree in July, 1946. His theological training he received at St. Mary's Seminary, Roland Park, Baltimore, Maryland, during the years 1946-1950. While there he acquired a Baccalaureate degree in Sacred Theology in June of 1948, and a Licentiate degree in Sacred Theology in June of 1950. He was ordained to the Sacred Priesthood in St. Mary's Cathedral, Trenton, New Jersey, on the Feast of Saints Peter and Paul, June 29, 1950. Following a temporary assignment as assistant pastor at St. Ann's Parish, Hampton, New Jersey, he was enrolled in the School of Canon Law at The Catholic University of America, where he received the Baccalaureate degree in Canon Law in June of 1951, and the Licentiate degree of Canon Law in June, 1952.

CANON LAW STUDIES *

337. Bourque, Rev. John R., S.T.L., J.C.L., The judicial power of the Church — Canon 1553, § 1

338. Cornell, Rev. Charles E., A.B., S.T.B., J.C.L., The juridical status of heretics and schismatics in good faith

339. Fitzgerald, Rev. William Francis, A. B., S.T.L., J.C.L., The parish census and the *liber status animarum*

340. Kubik, Rev. Stanislaus J., S.T.D., J. C. L., Invalidity of dispensations according to canon 84, § 1

341. Nugent, Rev. John Gerard, C.M., J. C. L., Ordination in societies of the common life

342. Peterson, Rev. Casimir Melvyn, S.S., A.B., S.T.L., J.C.L., Spiritual care in diocesan seminaries

343. Reiss, Rev. John Charles, A.B., S.T.L., J.C.L., The time and place of sacred ordination

344. Sheehan, Rev. Joseph George, J.C.L., The obligation of respect and obedience of clerics to their ordinary — Canon 127

345. Shekleton, Rev. Matthew M., O.S.M., J.C.L., Doctrinal Interpretation of law

346. Viau, Rev. Roger, S.T.L., J.C.L., Doubt in Canon Law

347. Walsh, Rev. Donnell Anthony, A.B., J. C. L., The new law on secular institutes

348. Sesto, Rev. Gennaro Joseph, S.D.B., A.B., S.T.L., Guardians of the mentally ill in ecclesiastical trials

349. Fus, Rev. Edward A., A.B., J.C.L., The extraordinary form of marriage according to canon 1098

* For a complete list of the available numbers of this series apply to the Catholic University of America Press, 620 Michigan Avenue, N.E., Washington (17), D. C.

www.ingramcontent.com/pod-product-compliance
Lightning Source LLC
LaVergne TN
LVHW050201080826
844660LV00012B/329

* 9 7 8 0 8 1 3 2 2 5 0 8 1 *